The New Americans
Recent Immigration and American Society

Edited by
Steven J. Gold and Rubén G. Rumbaut

A Series from LFB Scholarly

Homeland Conflict and Identity for Palestinian and Jewish Israeli Americans

Julianne Weinzimmer

LFB Scholarly Publishing LLC
El Paso 2011

Library of Congress Cataloging-in-Publication Data

Weinzimmer, Julianne Melissa, 1978-
Homeland conflict and identity for Palestinian and Jewish Israeli Americans / Julianne Weinzimmer.
p. cm. -- (The new Americans: recent immigration and American society)
Includes bibliographical references and index.
ISBN 978-1-59332-454-4 (hardcover : alk. paper)
1. Israelis--North Carolina. 2. Palestinian Arabs--North Carolina. 3. Arab-Israeli conflict--Social aspects--North Carolina. 4. Ethnic conflict. 5. Transnationalism. 6. East and West. 7. North Carolina--Ethnic relations. I. Title.
F265.I7W45 2011
305.8009756--dc22

2011002365

ISBN 978-1-59332-454-4

Printed on acid-free 250-year-life paper.

Manufactured in the United States of America.

Table of Contents

Acknowledgments

I gratefully thank Dr. Suzanne Shanahan, Dr. John Wilson, Dr. Edward Tiryakian, Dr. Eduardo Bonilla-Silva, Dr. Mary Hovsepian, and Dr. Rebecca Bach for their integral guidance and support.

I am indebted to my parents for giving me every opportunity in life to achieve my goals. Special thanks to the individuals of the RTP Palestinian and Jewish Israeli community who chose to share their inspiring life stories and perspectives with me.

This book is dedicated to Scott Wagar, who has accompanied me all along this long journey. Thank you for your time, dedication, and endless encouragement.

Introduction

This book is about how memories and narratives of conflict affect identity. More specifically, it is about how the ongoing conflict in Israel and the Israeli-occupied territories affects the identity of Jewish Israelis and Palestinians living in the United States. I argue that group conflict, even if it is not personally experienced, is a constitutive element of diasporic identity for both Jewish Israeli and Palestinian Americans. Through a series of twenty-nine in-depth interviews with both Jewish Israeli and Palestinian first and second generation immigrants, I identify the mechanisms through which perceptions of conflict affect identity. I assert that perceptions of violent conflict are independently significant in identity formation and maintenance processes.

The significance of this study is threefold. First is the timeliness of the study: the turbulent, violent history of this tiny piece of land has been a persistent object of international media coverage, and it continues to be a pressing global concern today. Second, the study uniquely looks at how conflict affects identity, despite the individual's distant location from the conflict. The study explores perceptions of conflict—derived from media coverage, personal connections, and other sources of information—and compares the effects that these perceptions have on Jewish Israeli American and Palestinian American identity. Third, while the maintenance of strong connections between the diaspora and the homeland has been well documented in Israeli and Palestinian literature, very little research has been done on the role that conflict and perceptions of conflict play in the creation and preservation of diasporic identity.

RESPONDING TO TILLY

In Charles Tilly's 2002 book, *Stories, Identities, and Political Change*, he claimed that identity stories and their salience are generated chiefly at the boundary between groups. Tilly viewed stories as a social construction—people tend to recall and reorganize their lived experiences as standard stories. He used these stories to better understand the social processes involved in creating and negotiating political entities and identities. The formation and sharing of stories accomplishes important social work, from promoting and justifying the actions of oneself and one's social group, to establishing order within social interactions and relations (Tilly, 2002, pp. 8-9). In regard to stories' specific functions for identity work, he claimed, "Standard stories locate identities within individual bodies as some combination of attribute, experience, and consciousness, then derive collective identities from the attributes, experiences, and consciousness shared by many individuals" (Tilly, 2002, p.10).

When discussing "boundary stories"—which group members use to delineate important differences between themselves and others—Tilly gave the specific example of divisions between Jews and Arabs, which become acute and standardized at the frontier between them, with identities becoming less defined away from the boundary (Tilly, 2002, p.11). I seek to demonstrate that identity is meaningfully affected not just by direct experience with boundary maintenance and interpersonal conflict, but also by *perceptions* of group-related conflict and discord, which are often gleaned from media depictions or shared narratives. While the manifest function of the conflict is for both groups to be able to claim the land of Israel/Palestine as the sole homeland for all Jews or Palestinians everywhere, a potential latent function is that this conflict works to increase the salience of diasporic identities by keeping people invested in and connected to the homeland.

THEORIZING ABOUT CONFLICT AND COMPETITION

Sociological analyses of ethnic conflict and identity have proliferated over the past four decades, as comprehensive research has been done on a variety of societies across the globe. My study, which pertains to issues of conflict between groups, relates directly to the founding insights of Georg Simmel. Simmel (1955) noted that inter-group conflict is socially significant in its latent function of promoting unity. Lewis Coser (1956) furthered Simmel's claims by examining a multitude of positive functions advanced by conflict—from bolstering group boundaries to preventing the departure of individuals from the group. The conflict over land and citizenship rights in Israel/Palestine makes both sides feel that their well-being and even existence is threatened. This facilitates greater collective identification, dependence, and conformity within each group, as well as tightening of boundaries and hostility towards the other side (Shamir & Sagiv-Schifter, 2006). The experience of being either the colonizer or the colonized, resulting in multidimensional social inequalities, also catalyzes the reinforcement of group divisions and identity (Memmi, 1965). I reveal some of the global implications of Coser and Simmel's theories by showing some of the many ways that homeland conflict helps keep the dispersed population united.

Fredrik Barth (1969) argued against simplistic social perspectives asserting that geographical and social isolation sustains cultural diversity. He empirically established that between-group interactions assist individuals in defining who they are by their perceived differences from others. Conflict between groups can result in the related identity superseding all others and becoming a dominant identity; it can also lead us to view social situations in dichotomous terms—outgroups and ingroups (Barth, 1969; Korostelina, 2007; Worchel, 2005). The continuous Palestinian-Israeli conflict is a frontier where group-level identity is distinguished through interactions with the "Other" (Barth, 1969). I argue that it influences each group's diasporic constituencies as well as those directly involved, since perceptions of conflict also play a critical role in diasporic identity. I use scholarly perspectives on how boundary-work builds community to illuminate why clear distinctions are drawn not just between Israelis and Palestinians, but also between Jews and Arabs throughout the world (Barth, 1969; Korostelina, 2007; Lamont & Molnar, 2002).

Conflict theorists (such as Barth, 1969; Simmel, 1955; and Olzak & Nagel, 1986) claim that ethnic identity, boundary maintenance, and internal organizational strength are promoted by competition and conflict. There are many instances of this: for example, the evolution of collective Palestinian identity after the British mandate (Hanafi, 2005; Khalidi, 1997) and panethnic Arab/Arab-American identity, which crystalized and became more salient after the 1967 Arab-Israeli war when Arab populations united through collective opposition to U.S. policy in the Middle East (Barghouti, 1988; Gold & Bozorgmehr, 2007; Shain, 1996). The dispute over land, including territory in Israel/Palestine, also incited the creation in 1964 of the Palestine Liberation Organization (PLO), which only came to be seen by the U.S. and other nations as a legitimate representative of the Palestinian plight beginning in 1988 (Barghouti, 1988; Bishara, 2008; Shain, 1996). The victory of the PLO in obtaining an official response—the withdrawal of Israeli troops from the occupied territory of Gaza in late summer, 2005—demonstrates how their organizational strength led to outside recognition and political power.

Competition theory maintains that ethnic violence and collective action are most prevalent during episodes of increased competition between groups, and also when ethnic inequalities begin to break down (Olzak and Nagel, 1986; Olzak, 1992). This trend is apparent amongst my populations in three main ways. First, it is observable in the Israeli-Palestinian violence constantly erupting over nationhood and ethnic inequalities in the form of citizenship rights. Both sides of the conflict endured sustained periods of bloodshed during the two *Intifadas* (Palestinian uprisings) and also shorter bursts of violent encounters, most commonly in the form of Israeli military invasions seeking out Palestinian militants, riots and protests on both sides, missile launches, and suicide bombings.

Second, it is seen in the preservation of Palestinian identity and group solidarity within and beyond national borders. The Palestinian cause is as a fundamental foundation for panethnic Arab identity in the United States and Israel thus serves as an antagonist that fosters Arab-American solidarity (Gold & Bozorgmehr, 2007; Shain, 1996). Several pan-ethnic organizations have been created on both sides to preserve connections to the diaspora in the U.S. and to promote their continued assistance to those still in the homeland. Examples of Jewish Israeli American organizations that foster pan-Israeli/Jewish identity and connectivity are Hadassah, The Jewish Federation, and The American Israel Public Affairs Committee (AIPAC). Two examples of Palestinian American groups that serve this function are the Arab American Institute (AAI) and the Arab American Anti-Discrimination Committee (ADC).

It is thirdly seen in the increased demands made on behalf of Palestinians as Israel has made greater concessions over time (such as the aforementioned 2005 disengagement plan in Gaza). I relate the competition theory to my conflict research by analyzing how ethnic solidarity necessitates both identification with this particular ascribed status and the maintenance of strong ethnic networks—here in the form of diasporic connections between the homeland and the United States.

THE CONTEXT OF THE CONFLICT

To analyze the effects that conflict has on identity, one must first situate the conflict within a historical context, thus demonstrating how conflict is shaped by the time period in which it occurs (Rumbaut, 2002). The long history of ethnic and political tensions between Israelis and Palestinians has facilitated highly visible conflict and a collective fear for safety within each group. International media coverage of the conflict is broad and includes events in major Israeli cities (Haifa, Tel Aviv, and Jerusalem) and in occupied territories (Gaza and the West Bank) such as bus and car bombings and other terrorist attacks, military-related violence, political conflict, and riots and demonstrations in public spaces.

With the inception of the modern State of Israel in 1948, the ancient Jewish belief that God ordained Palestine for them came to fruition, from the Jewish perspective (Davies, 1982; Peled, 1992). The nation was also declared a safe home protecting all Jews and their descendants from anti-Semitism and persecution, a response to the recent Holocaust (Peled, 1992). Israel as a sovereign state became an important symbol of Jewish solidarity and identity for Jews in the diaspora, who were guaranteed a home in Israel through the "law of return" and the "law of citizenship" (Don-Yehiya, 1998). The establishment of a new nation also resulted in the creation of over 700,000 Palestinian refugees, based on United Nations Relief and Work Agency for Palestinian Refugees (UNRWA) estimates (Hammer, 2005). The relatively recent loss of their country, which they refer to as the *nakba* ("catastrophe"), is a salient collective memory among the Palestinian diaspora; it unites them as they live dispersed in exile from their historic homeland, without a territory to which they can return (Eastmond, 2007; Hammer, 2005; Levinson & Ember, 1997).

An additionally important historical factor relates to the power relations and divisions created between the colonizer and the colonized. Group-level divisions, distinctions, and identity effects become more salient through the process of colonization and conflict over land and civil rights (Memmi, 1965; Simmel, 1955). Scholars have sought to examine how the colonizer can impose meaning or identities on the colonized, and how the interrelations and violence between the two shape identity (Berezin, 1997; Memmi, 1965). In investigating what life under colonization looks like for Palestinians, it is important to grasp how economic and political exploitation has facilitated extreme disparity between Israel and the Gaza Strip and West Bank. In order to illustrate this point, I turn to statistics reported by the Central Intelligence Agency World Factbook. The population of Gaza was estimated as of July, 2010 to be 1,604,238 living on 360 square kilometers, and West Bank estimates were 2,514,845 people living on 5,860 square kilometers of land. The unemployment rate as of 2009 was 40% for Gaza and 19% for the West Bank, and roughly 70% and 46% of these two populations respectively are living below the poverty line. In comparison to the 4,119,083 Palestinians living on just over 6,000 square kilometers, the population of Israel is around 7,353,985 people living on 22,072 square kilometers (based on 2007 reports, this includes roughly 187,000 Israeli settlers in the West Bank, about 20,000 in the occupied territory of the Golan Heights, and less than 177,000 in the Arab section, East Jerusalem). While the average GDP per capita for both Gaza and the West Bank was $2,900 in American dollars as of 2008, it was $28,900 in Israel. The unemployment rate in Israel was 7.6% and 23.6% lived below the poverty line.

Communities need to be situated and understood within concrete historical contexts, as they are influenced by past relations between sending and receiving countries. Both Palestinians and Jewish Israelis/Jews collectively recall a history of victimization, persecution, and denial of rights. These memories remain salient for group unity and identity, especially considering their continuous violent experiences with each other. Despite these commonalities, the international response to each group has differed. While the Zionist political project was successful in receiving worldwide recognition of their right to reclaim their ancestral land of Israel, Palestinians have always struggled for legitimacy and acknowledgement from the outside world (Bishara, 2008; Ellis, 2002; Khalidi, 1997). The trend of anti-Arab (including anti-Palestinian) sentiment in the U.S. has been heavily discussed by scholars and social theorists (Ackerman, 2001; Barghouti, 1988; Chomsky, 2010; Dunsky, 2008; Ellis, 2009; Gold & Bozorgmehr, 2007; Khalidi, 1997; Marvasti & McKinney, 2004; Portes

& Rumbaut, 2006; Shain, 1996; Said, 1979). Its modern roots have been identified with the U.S. decision to align itself with Israel in the aftermath of the 1967 war (Marvasti & McKinney, 2004). It notably escalated following the events of September 11th, 2001, when the words "Arab," "Muslim," and "terrorist" became treated as synonymous at both the individual level as well as the institutional level, as evidenced by media representations and policies such as the USA PATRIOT Act (El-Aswad, 2006; Ellis, 2009, Gillespie, 2006; Gold & Bozorgmehr, 2007; Marvasti & McKineey, 2004; Matar, 2006; Noakes & Wilkins, 2002; Portes & Rumbaut, 2006; Talbot, 2008). As I demonstrate, particularly in Chapter Four, which focuses on participants' experiences in the United States, these factors are of great import for diasporic individuals' identities, as their self-concepts are shaped by experiences with discrimination and either acceptance or delegitimization in the host country.

DEFINING "DIASPORA"

I use the term "diaspora" and refer to "diasporic identity" in my research because while the original term referred to expulsion from a homeland and being socially marginalized in a receiving country while return is awaited, it is now used to describe those exiled or displaced to a number of different nation-states by a variety of economic, political, and social forces (Levitt, 2001). Rogers Brubaker (2005) argued that the three main characteristics of a diaspora are physical dispersion, homeland orientation, and the maintenance of group boundaries. In her attempt to clarify the concept of diaspora, Robin Cohen (1997) identified the criteria involved:

> …dispersal or travel from an original homeland to two or more foreign regions; a collective memory or myth of an idealized homeland; a commitment to the maintenance of the homeland, including a movement for return; a strong, long-term group consciousness and identity; a belief in a shared fate; a range of possible relations (from troubling to enriching) with the host society; and finally, a sense of empathy and solidarity with coethnics in other places of settlement. (as cited in Gold, 2002, p. 2)

Both Brubaker and Cohen's definitions apply to Palestinians and Jews (the archetypal diaspora group) and also to Israeli emigrants. The term "diaspora" works well to encapsulate how these constituencies retain ties with the homeland and have their identities shaped by homeland conflict. Although Israelis may not count as a traditional diaspora per se because of the brief length of their exile and their ability to return, they have been socialized in Israel, are intimately acquainted with the language of diaspora, and frequently use this term to describe their identity and experiences (Gold, 2002). It has even been argued that are a "double diaspora" because they are both Jewish and Israeli and thus have two distinct histories and sets of characteristics (Rebhun & Lev Ari, 2010). Despite condemnation received from Israel (which perceives out-migration as threatening to the ideological and demographic viability of the Jewish State), and despite their typically successful assimilation in the host country, Israeli emigrants retain strong connections with the homeland, adopting transnational social patterns and continuously longing for and visiting it (Cohen & Gold, 1996; Gold, 1997, 2002, 2007; Rebhun & Lev Ari, 2010). The same feelings towards the country of origin and basic patterns exist for the Palestinian diaspora, except for the crucial element of being able to frequently visit (Hanafi, 2005). Both ethnic groups are thus commonly viewed as diasporas as well as a transnational migrant population, since they are building their lives in one land while identifying with another (Gold, 2002, 2007; Hammer, 2005; Levitt & Waters, 2002; Portes & Rumbaut, 2006; Rebhun & Lev Ari, 2010, Stein & Swedenburg, 2005).

CONCEPTUALIZING "IDENTITY"

I do not conceive of social identity as a static, objective "thing" to be discovered that involves rigidity and sameness among group members. Instead, I align myself with Tilly (1996), who imagined identity as necessarily flexible for a social constructivist approach, yet "hard" enough to do useful theoretical work (Brubaker & Cooper, 2000, p. 12). There is hybridity in identity—it is simultaneously dynamic and fixed (Easthope, 2009). I am using "identity" to refer to the "unstable, multiple, fluctuating, and fragmented nature of the contemporary 'self'," as it relates to a sense of belonging to a bounded group—a mix between "identification" and "commonality" (Brubaker & Cooper, 2000, p. 8). Identity is a socially-constructed process, where the individual varyingly focuses on "…language and narrative as communicative vehicles of identity" (Berezin, 1997, p. 21), and, as Richard Jenkins' (2008) suggested, all identities are social identities, since identity formation and maintenance always involves social interactions. Such perspectives also note that identity, as it relates to ethnic group membership, has a "volitional dimension," where the individual's own background leads him or her to choose how and to what degree he or she identifies with the group (Nagel, 1996, p. 20). Social identity serves as a link between individual thought processes and the structures and processes of large social groups (Korostelina, 2007).

Patterson (2006, p. 1896) discussed how among the multitude of social identities individuals in the diaspora simultaneously maintain, racially/ethnically-based identities, and the socialization around them, affect the core of the self more than "transitory identities" such as professional status. This socialization occurs around emotionally-intense and influential issues, such as common ancestry, extended kinship networks, and collective myth experiences, which all further encourage group solidarity. As is the case with any other social identity, ethnic identities involve ingroup-outgroup perspectives, whereby individuals come to view themselves as similar to and aligned with one social category as compared to another. As Stets and Burke (2000) have noted, these social categories precede the individual; a person derives her or his sense of self and role expectations from the structure of society. However, agency is also involved in the process, as ethnic self-identification includes situationally-based feelings that can vary over time and by place or surroundings (Zimmermann, Zimmermann, & Constant, 2007).

I derive from this multitude of perspectives a complex reconceptualization of the term "identity" and I use it in my exploration of diasporic identity as an ongoing process that is mediated by individual-level perceptions of conflict. Recognizing the complexity and multiplicity involved in diasporic identity, I turn to Rashid Khalidi, who asserted that a possible pitfall in studying Palestinian identity is the

> …tendency to see an essential Palestinian identity going well back in time, rather than the complex, contingent, and relatively recent reality of Palestinian identity, and to stress factors of unity at the expense of those tending toward

> fragmentation or diversity in Palestinian society and politics. (1997, p. 34)

As the State of Israel is also relatively new and its population is extremely diverse and multifaceted, Khalidi's counsel is useful for examining the identities of the Israeli diaspora as well.

Transnationalism and Identity

It is also important to look at the transnational dimensions involved in identity processes. Olzak and Nagel (1986) maintain that the forces of modernization spark ethnic movements, for example in the creation of transnational and migrant communities. Globalization and time-space compression, in the forms of increased worldwide travel, dissemination of information, and communication, has permanently altered the ties between space and place (Georgiou, 2006; Gowricharn, 2009; Haller & Landolt, 2005; Portes & Rumbaut, 2006). These changes have created new possibilities for transnational and multiple identities and communities, and thus they have had an immense impact on the way identity—including that of Israeli Americans (Gold, 2007) and Palestinian Americans (Georgiou, 2006)—is conceived. Extensive research on transnationalism has shown that migrant families continue to orient certain parts of their new lives around the sending country—they maintain their social ties there and (when possible) travel back and forth (Georgiou, 2006; Gold 2007; Haller & Landolt, 2005; Patterson, 2006; Portes & Rumbaut, 2005, 2006; Rebhun & Lev Ari, 2010; Waldinger & Fitzgerald, 2004; Zimmermann et al., 2006).

In my analyses, I incorporate important insights from critiques by Waldinger and Fitzgerald (2004) and Zimmermann et al. (2007), who have noted that previous studies tend to define transnationalism in terms of regular and sustained activities and view the attachments to both host and home country as mutually exclusive. These authors have argued that several prior transnationalism studies have ignored variance and multiplicity in individuals' connectivity between host and home countries. Such variations exist for several reasons, including the interaction between the migrant population and state politics, both in the host and home country (Gold & Bozorgmehr, 2007; Hanafi, 2005; Sakr, 1999; Wald, 2009; Waldinger & Fitzgerald, 2004), and the fact that ethnic self-identification can shift across time, space, and life circumstances (Zimmermann et al., 2007). Waldinger and Fitzgerald (2004) stressed the need for a wider range of studies in this area of transnationalism, as the limited sample of cases thus far considered makes the range of connectivity possibilities difficult to assess. Transnationalism involves numerous linkages occurring across multiple settings at both macro- and micro-levels, including demographic, political, economic, cultural, and familial factors (Gold, 1997). Some of the specific multi-level factors that matter for this study, as I will demonstrate, are related to generational status, shifting perspectives across the lifecourse, and power differentials between Palestinians and Israelis in areas such as entry and exit in the homeland, citizenship laws, and national belonging.

Several scholars (Kasinitz, Waters, Mollenkopf, & Anil, 2002; Kibria, 2002; Levitt, 2009; Rumbaut, 2002) have incorporated transnational migration perspectives into studies of second generation immigrants' attachment to their parents' homeland and the influence of these transnational connections on identity. The second generation of the second wave of immigrants to the United States (those arriving since the Immigration Act of 1965, mainly since the 1980s) is still relatively young and is the fastest growing segment of the U.S. population under the age of 18; therefore, their transnational practices constitute an area to be explored by novel research (Levitt & Waters, 2002). I use transnationalism theory and literature to examine how the identities of the second generation are differentially affected by homeland conflict as compared to the first generation. While Levitt (2009, p. 1226) agreed with the bulk of immigration literature which suggests that the second generation are not as regularly or deeply attached as the first (Gans, 2007; Kasinitz et al., 2002; Kibria, 2002; Rumbaut, 2002; Waters, Tran, Kasinitz, & Mollenkopf, 2010), she also argued, as do I, that this should not lead scholars to dismiss the potentially important impact of being raised in a transnational social environment. Even if the second generation do not visit the homeland or speak the language, they are still often raised in homes where the country of origin is referenced ideologically and materially on a daily basis and have been socialized by transnationally-active individuals (Levitt & Jaworsky, 2007; Levitt, 2009). As Patterson (2006) acknowledged, diasporic or transnational ties can be as concrete as individuals dispersed from but still connected to the home country, or they can be based on an ideological, collective myth about a homeland that a person has never even visited, much less lived in. Patterson also noted that a transnational community member who has never lived in the sending country can have even stronger feelings about supporting the homeland than someone who was born there. This is especially true when the homeland situation involves conflict and a perceived adversary, as is the situation in Israel/Palestine.

Forces of modernization and the resulting transnational ties assist both the Jewish Israeli and Palestinian diaspora in retaining connections to homeland conflict. These connections are especially maintained via transnational social networks, pan-ethnic group organizations, and prominent international media reportage (Portes & Rumbaut, 2006). These and other aforementioned insights assist me in modifying and extending Tilly's (2002) claim that conflict influences identity predominantly at the boundary, by showing that perceptions of conflict from within the diaspora can and do have real identity effects.

METHODOLOGICAL MODELS

Narratives and Accounts

One of the major ways I explore boundary-work and diasporic identity is through examining narratives/accounts and collective/social memories derived from in-depth interviews. In explaining my choice to use open-ended interviews, I rely on the insights of Bonilla-Silva (2003), who argued that this method best helps us understand individuals' beliefs as they are produced and reproduced through communication and social interaction. I agree with his assertion that surveys are less useful than interviews in explaining the "how" and "why" involved in the development of ideologies, and that they tend to confine and guide interview responses. In my own analyses, I discovered that while several individuals I interviewed described themselves as not having biases against the Other, they would later reveal their true feelings by discussing each other in terms of crude categorizations and mass stereotypes.

I assert, akin to Dhunpath (2000), that our lives and the way we represent our experiences are "intrinsically narrative in quality" (p. 545). Following the methodological undertakings of multiple scholars (Bonilla-Silva, 2003; Dhunpath, 2000; Olick & Robbins, 1998; Orbuch, 1997; Tilly, 2002), I use subjects' personal stories, also referred to in sociology literature as "accounts" or "narratives," and their socially-shared memories as a way to examine the process by which perceptions of distant conflict affect identity.

Storytelling and accounts are used by sociologists and anthropologists as a methodological means to understand people's ideological beliefs as well as how they conceive of the social world. Accounts are useful for apprehending the human experience, the development of collective meanings, and common understandings of other ethnic groups (Orbuch, 1997). We use stories daily as a way to communicate to others and reinforce for ourselves our understanding of the social structure and our location within it. These stories thus cumulatively work to reinforce societal order in a subtle way. In the case of the Palestinian-Israeli conflict, I found this notion to be true, as my subjects used stories about homeland conflict to explain to me why their own group should be viewed as the victim while the opposing group is the aggressor and wrong-doer.

Social and Collective Memory

As Orbuch (1997, p. 465) mentioned in her discussion of accounts and narratives, it has been theorized that although stories are mainly recollections of past events, they also influence the way individuals currently see themselves and others. In the process of creating a dominant group narrative and collective memories, individuals' own recollections of the past may fuse with those of others while they simultaneously incorporate elements from prevailing historical accounts (Eastmond, 2007; Misztal, 2010). This is the crucial link connecting my use of storytelling/account methods with social memory theory as a methodological tool.

The field of collective memory, including the groundbreaking work of Maurice Halbwachs, has been greatly informed by Durkheimian sociology, especially in concepts such as collective conscience and commemorative rituals (Beim, 2007; Olick, 1999, 2008). In *On Collective Memory* (1992), Halbwachs' seminal piece, he made a key distinction between actual history and collective memory—while history remains in the past, collective memories are the active past which forms our identities. Each social group has its own collective memory upon which it continuously draws as it selectively reconstructs the past (Yerushalmi, 1982; Keightley, 2010). Burke (1989) warned that failing to pay attention to the collective leads us to ignore the important ways that we are influenced by the groups to which we belong. Noting this, I look for common themes in the stories of the past told to me by my subjects. As I discuss in Chapter One, one major trend was for subjects from both sides of the conflict to refer to historical trends of persecution (i.e., the Holocaust, or the displacement of the Palestinians in 1948 and 1967) as a way of explaining why the conflict over land rights is so important to them and their people.

Halbwachs (1992) also noted that via social memories we can participate in the past and make it important for our own lives, even if we have not directly experienced it. Family, he says, assists us as we learn to construct the past and acquire social identities. We acquire stories from our parents that teach us about the external world and what it means to be a part of the group. We not only recount or listen to familial stories and memories—we also reminisce about their meaning, evaluate, and interpret them (Fivush, 2008; Keightley, 2010). Identity formation is especially about values imparted by family and community (Langfield, 2009). Orbuch (1997, p. 472) discussed how accounts—like social memories—are learned in the same ways as other social behaviors: from parents, peers, and other social institutions (i.e., religious organizations and the media). I confirmed this pattern of acquisition in my own analyses. In the next chapter I reveal the highly discernable impact that parents' stories about homeland conflict have on the identities of the second generation.

The choice to use collective memories of the conflict as a way to examine diasporic identity stems from the following claims of Chamberlain and Leydesdorff (2004):

> Migrants, perhaps more than many people, are made by their memories of their birthplace, their homeland, those left behind . . . For the most part, however, migrant memories are not part of the regular scientific tool kit for studying migration and those transnational families whose lives straddle two or more nation-states… (p. 228)

My study answers this implicit call for research on how shared memories of the homeland impact transnational and diasporic identities.

In summary, I rely on central ideas from all of these literatures—narratives, social memory, transnationalism, and identity—to explain, through the use of accounts, the ways by which homeland conflict continues to matter for group members who have migrated to the United States. I also use these theories and methods to elucidate how the identities of second generation members, some of whom have never even visited the homeland, continue to be affected by the conflict there.

THE SAMPLE

Deciding Who to Study

Nancy Foner (2009) lauded the benefits of a comparative approach in migration studies, as it allows the researcher to recognize and highlight important dynamics that may be overlooked if only one case is analyzed. Noting this, I decided to interview both groups involved in the conflict in an effort to disentangle the effect distant conflict has on identity. Interviewing both first and second generation immigrants from each ethnic group permitted me to analyze the possible linkages between each group's history of violence and their current relationship with conflict. One of my initial interests was whether or not the individual's sense of being a Jew or a Palestinian, in relation to the conflict in Israel/Palestine, is somehow linked to her or his group's collective, long-term history of persecution and conflict. Examples of this history of violence include the creation and establishment of ghettos across Europe and the Holocaust as collective memories of the Jews, and the history of colonization as collective memories of the Palestinians. As I expected, these connections between past and current conflict did exist in the minds of my subjects. This is one of the major themes of Chapter One. I chose to interview members of both populations involved in this conflict in order to capture the entire story of how the Israeli-Palestinian conflict affects diaspora constituents. This decision also assisted me in overcoming my own bias and limited perspective as a Jewish American who has visited and lived in Israel for a cumulative period of about a year and a half. (I return in more detail below, as well as in the Conclusion and Appendix, to the issues of my potential interpretive biases and possible influences on interview responses.)

In gathering my sample, I followed specific guidelines that I developed, which detail who is considered to be a Jewish Israeli American or a Palestinian American for the purposes of my study. There are three ways to become a Jewish Israeli: move to Israel from another country and make *aliyah* (become a citizen officially), be born there (which makes the person a *sabra*), or be born outside of Israel to Israeli parents (Gold, 2002, p. 22). As Gold explained, this definition of who counts as Israeli is transnational in that it reflects the proliferation of migrants worldwide who preserve connections to their homeland while living in another. Gold also noted the unique complexities involved in Israeli citizenship, since while some migrants in Israel are technically citizens of their country of birth, they see themselves and are seen by Israeli leaders as Israeli, and can thus also be viewed as Israeli emigrants when they leave the country.

I decided to emulate Gold's (2002) method used in his study of Israeli emigrants in America, defining Israeli émigrés as those who identify themselves as such. However, due to the nature of my research, I decided to also add one caveat based on Gold's claim that short-term residents (such as tourists, students, and visiting scholars) tend to isolate themselves within émigré communities. I wanted to focus on the perceptions of individuals who have been distanced from the conflict, and so I only included self-identified first and second generation Israeli immigrants who: 1) are not short-term residents but intend to build a life in America without any firm plans to return to Israel, and 2) have lived in the United States for at least six months.

Palestinians are a very different case, as they are officially stateless and were widely dispersed (mostly across the Middle East and to a lesser extent across the United States and throughout the world) as a result of the 1948 and 1967 occupation of their land and homes. In deciding who to include in my Palestinian sample, I again included individuals who self-identify as first or second generation Palestinian, since the only technical Palestinian identification comes from having UNRWA refugee status or living in the occupied territories. And again, I included the two specific criteria listed above for my Israeli sample in order to ensure that these individuals are indeed Palestinian-Americans and not merely visitors.

Drawing the Sample

The subject sample used for this study has been drawn from one community—the area referred to as the Research Triangle of North

Carolina (including cities Chapel Hill, Raleigh, and Durham).[1] It is not random or nationally representative, although I have attempted to include as much individual-level variation as is possible, given the well-articulated constraints of a community study (Levitt, 2001). I cannot generalize my results to the United States population with any degree of statistical confidence, and instead my goal has been to conduct an in-depth, inductive examination of the conflict perceptions and resulting identity effects of a diverse community sample.

My sample was drawn over the course of 2006 and 2007 through the snowball method, using the many contacts I made to people connected to and involved in the local Jewish and Palestinian communities.[2] I made contact with several Triangle synagogues, mosques, ethnic food restaurants, campus groups, ethnic organizations, and social networks. This multitude of contacts allowed me to obtain a sample of twenty-nine individuals who are diverse in important areas such as education, age, religion, occupation, and connections to homeland conflict. This sample variance is imperative if I want to have results that reflect the actual Research Triangle population. The final sample consisted of nine first generation and six second generation Jewish Israeli Americans, and five first generation and nine second generation Palestinian Americans. (I have created a table of descriptive

---

[1] This region, named for the high-tech Research Triangle Park, is home to three major research universities and has a total population of approximately 1.2 million. The median household income is $56,014 and 48.2% of the population has earned a bachelor's or higher degree (averages based on 2006-2008 U.S. Census data for the region's three main counties: Wake County, Durham County, and Orange County).

[2] Data on the region's Israeli and Palestinian immigrant populations are difficult to come by, but for the entire State of North Carolina, the 2000 U.S. Census lists 1,764 people reporting Palestinian ancestry (compared with a U.S. total of 72,112) and only 745 individuals reporting Israeli ancestry (compared with a U.S. total of 106,839) (State of North Carolina Ancestry Data). For various reasons, actual figures for those identifying as members of the two groups are likely to be somewhat higher, but in any case the local population percentages of both groups are probably quite small (though this more densely-populated and economically-prosperous metropolitan region of the state is likely home to a fairly significant share of the state's total population of members of the two groups).

demographics detailing the most integral characteristics of my sample. Table 1 can be found beginning on page 173.)

Locating individuals was a daunting but not impossible task. It was easier to locate first generation Jewish Israelis and second generation Palestinians than second generation Jewish Israelis and first generation Palestinians. First generation Jewish Israelis were much easier to find and identify, due to their frequently higher rate of group associations and community visibility than the more typically assimilated members of the second generation. As expected, first generation Palestinians were more difficult to locate, due to factors such as language barriers and scarcity in the community.

Additionally, as I had anticipated, it was more difficult to locate first generation Palestinians because of trust issues. I was warned by Palestinians I initially spoke with that it would be a challenge to get members of the Palestinian population to speak with me, due to their fears of giving me their names and consequently experiencing racial profiling, and their wariness of my own potential biases as a Jewish American. "Hassan,"[3] the man with whom I conducted a life history, told me that especially since the events of September 11th, 2001, Palestinian Americans are hesitant to be active in Palestinian groups or talk about homeland issues. I took great measures to establish a trusting relationship with the respondents, mostly by relying on previously interviewed Palestinians to speak on my behalf and make initial contact for me. I also worked hard to ensure that everyone was confident about the validity and confidentiality of my study.

Reflecting on the Researcher Role

This study examines how conflict involving one's group affects the identity of those who live far away from the conflict site. I assert that my background makes me an ideal candidate for researching this important topic, since I have lived across Israel and interacted with both Israelis and Palestinians.

Robert Merton (1972) discussed the important distinctions between "Insiders" and "Outsiders" in relation to social scientists studying groups and accessing knowledge. Extreme Insiderism posits that one must be a member of the group in order to examine it; having been

---

[3] All subjects' names have been changed to ethnically appropriate pseudonyms to protect their identities. All ages and background details reflect respondents' statuses at the time of the interviews, which were conducted in 2006 and 2007.

socialized within the group, the Insider thus knows which issues matter. The opposite end of the spectrum, Outsiderism, holds that Insiders tend to glorify the in-group and thus cannot avoid ethnocentrism and chauvinism, particularly during times of intense social conflict between groups. Merton concluded that in reality, the boundaries between being an Insider and an Outsider are more permeable than these doctrines allow for, and agreed with Mannheim (1952) that some intellectuals can be a part of both categories, by having diverse social backgrounds and by not subscribing to a particular side of the conflict (Merton, 1972, p. 29). Simmel (1955) noted that refraining from claiming allegiances to either group helps one remain more objective.

I demonstrate support for Mannheim's claims, as I am partially a member of one of the groups I am studying, being Jewish, but am also an Outsider in that I have intensely studied both sides of the conflict and do not maintain a position favoring either side. Being a partial Insider for one of the groups assists me in having greater insights on intra-group relations and conceptualizations as I create a "thick" description of Israelis' diasporic experiences (Geertz, 1973). Being an Outsider who is not directly tied into the conflict helps me both to listen more objectively to my subjects as they explain their viewpoints on the Israeli-Palestinian conflict, and to work to draw unbiased conclusions related to their ethnic identities. Although I maintain that my own history and position makes me well-suited for researching this topic, I do take the advice and precautions of Keightley (2010) into great consideration. She calls for researcher reflexivity in order to ensure rigor, noting that one must be constantly aware of her or his social and cultural location in relation to participants. Both data and analyses are affected by the personal characteristics of both subject and researcher, such as ethnicity, gender, and age.

While I never volunteered information about my Jewish background, I did not deny it if asked. In addition, because my last name is commonly viewed as "sounding Jewish," there is a good chance that many subjects made a presumption. Respondents' knowledge or assumptions of my background may have affected interview responses, for example, possibly hindering Palestinian subjects' willingness to express more intensely negative feelings or characterizations about Jews or Jewish Israelis. Conversely, perceptions of my background may have led Jewish Israelis to feel more comfortable expressing similar types of views about Palestinians.

Bearing these possibilities in mind, as well as pondering other unanticipated researcher effects, I looked for and sought to acknowledge such instances if and when they appeared to arise. While my religious/cultural background may introduce an additional variable to the interview process, I maintain that it does not invalidate my analyses or conclusions. I also note, once again, that my partial Insider status put me in a unique position to better understand and appreciate the complexities involved in relating to this conflict from within the diaspora. For those interested, I reflect in Appendix B on my own feelings and experiences related to this research project and these interviews (see page 165).

THE STRUCTURE OF THE STUDY

Beginning with Oral Histories

I began the process by conducting two life histories, one with a first generation Palestinian American and one with a first generation Jewish Israeli American. Keightley (2010) argued that the unstructured format of oral histories, with the researcher introducing themes and prompts, gives the subject space to both explore and express remembered experiences in greater depth than other methodologies. This methodological approach also gives the researcher abundant, detailed data which highlights the role of memories in migrant experiences and self-concepts (Chamberlain & Leydesdorff, 2004). I used information garnered from the life histories to construct my main interview questionnaire. A copy of the interview questionnaire can be found in Appendix A, beginning on page 159.

Another reason I chose to begin my interviews with life histories involved an important insight from Olick and Robbins (1998), who discussed how oral historians view their enterprise as a democratic one, a means of giving history and a voice —and thus power —back to the people involved. My aim here is to understand the conflict from the viewpoints of those involved, thus going beyond media generalizations and stereotyping. As Dhunpath (2000) put it,

> Insight . . . is best achieved by trying to understand how life is seen by those living it rather than by accepting uncritically perspectives of those administering the system. . . . We have to change the established canon of research to give audience to marginalized voices. (p. 550)

Marita Eastmond (2007) has added that because many refugee situations involved ambiguity and oftentimes the dominant narrative comes from the group with greater overall power, it becomes especially important for refugee stories to be heard and believed. Esposito and Murphy (2000) also argued that storytelling—a central methodological framework employed throughout this study—has the emancipatory capacity to give minority populations a chance to represent themselves through their own words. As Juliane Hammer (2005) acknowledged in her study of Palestinians in exile, the researcher can never completely transcend the process whereby subjects' stories become a means of making arguments and drawing conclusions; however, the underlying goal remains "…to let my interviewees speak for themselves, to give them a voice through my own discursive power" (p. 8).

Chapter Organization

In Chapter One, I examine how subjects from both ethnic groups utilize collective memories and dominant narratives about their people's historical experiences with oppression, discrimination, and violence to frame the current conflict in the homeland and their continuous relationship with it from within the diaspora. In this chapter as well as the following chapters, I look for parallels and differences both between ethnic groups overall and between generations within and across ethnic boundaries.

In Chapter Two, I employ the same methodologies to explore how respondents use personal conflict narratives or shared family memories to make sense of the ongoing conflict and its impact on their diasporic identities. Literature on perceptions of the Palestinian-Israeli conflict (Barghouti, 1988; Ellis, 2002; Grossman, 1993; Khalidi, 1997; Khalili, 2005; Roy, 1995; Said, 1979; Stein & Swedenburg, 2005; Uslaner, Canetti-Nisim & Pedazhur, 2004) led me to expect what my results confirmed, that Israelis and Palestinians define conflict in dissimilar ways. Conflict for an Israeli more often takes the form of a bus bombing or military-related violence, while for a Palestinian it is more centered on the military usurpation of homes and land, and forms of inequality related to personal rights, such as denial of access to work or border patrol harassment. These experiences were the bases of Palestinians' conceptualizations of homeland conflict—for them it was something that dominates their daily lives and is unavoidable.

Chapter Three explores sources of information about homeland conflict and how they shape identity. It has been noted that mainstream, international mass media mold attitudes and that coverage of Israel/Palestine centers on and exaggerates violence and inter-group conflict (Ackerman, 2001; Dunsky, 2008; Ellis, 2009; Kamalipour, 1997; Noakes & Wilkins, 2002). I expected respondents to generally rely on two main sources of information about homeland conflict: personal networks and American or international media. It was thus logical to assume that the groups would differentially conceive of and be affected by homeland conflict, not just based on generational differences in actually experiencing homeland conflict, but also because of the dissimilar ways that the conflict is typically discussed in Palestinian and Jewish Israeli literature, by the family, and in public discourse.

The central theme of Chapter Four is respondents' experiences with and relationships within the host country, and the effect these have on how distant conflict shapes identity. The two groups' transnational experiences differ based on their encounters with and within the United States. This is due to factors such as the exclusively Jewish right of return to the homeland, America's identification as a key player in the peace process and ideologically pro-Zionist, and negative portrayals of Arabs in the media and popular culture. As Zimmermann et al. (2007) and Gans (2007) have both noted, ethnic self-identification can be partially imposed upon someone, depending on the way the dominant culture of a society labels a particular ethnic group. Georgiou (2006) adds that identity is not solely a cultural process but is also politically influenced, since issues of power, hegemony, and exclusion also matter.

All of these central themes—collective memories of persecution, conflict experiences within the homeland, media and alternative information use, and divergent encounters within America—work to contextualize my intergenerational assessment of how perceptions of conflict in the homeland affect Jewish Israeli American and Palestinian American identity. This novel exploration uses insights gathered from one community to explore far larger, substantial sociological phenomena related to transnationalism, conflict, and ethnic identity.

CHAPTER 1:

Collective Memories about the Foundations of the Conflict

I begin this chapter with a brief discussion of how theories on collective memory and storytelling can serve as mechanisms for assessing how homeland conflict affects identity. I apply these methods to my interview data, paying particular attention to the different ways memories and narratives work depending on ethnic group and generational status. What I discover is that the historical antecedents of the ongoing Palestinian-Israeli conflict are part of subjects' common discourse used to frame their own diasporic lives and identities.

SOCIAL AND COLLECTIVE MEMORY

Beginning in the early '80s with the rise of multiculturalism, academia and the general public were inundated with references to social and collective memory (Olick & Robbins, 1998). Within sociology there was a shift from analyzing social structures to "practice," moving beyond seeing culture as the classical functionalist triad of norms, values, and attitudes by also noting its foundational role underlying all social processes (Olick & Robbins, 1998). Social memory—a theoretical tool I use to understand the ongoing process by which homeland conflict affects diasporic identity—thus fits well into the reorientation of cultural sociology.

Collective memory is the past in action, and through it we can relate to that which we have not experienced directly, thus keeping the past alive (Halbwachs, 1992). Schwartz (1996) used the metaphor of a mirror and a lamp to explain how collective memory goes beyond merely reflecting our past by orienting us—it is both a model *of* and a model *for* society. I will discuss subjects' collectively-held memories, which are passed down from parent to child, and show how these recollections demonstrate to current and future generations that caring and being informed about homeland conflict is an integral part of belonging for both groups.

Of course, there are differences in how these shared memories mediate the process by which homeland conflict affects diasporic identity, not just by ethnic group membership but also depending on generational status. Having experienced violence and threat firsthand has a different long-term impact on a person than simply hearing about it. These distinctions are the crux of this chapter.

FIRST GENERATION JEWISH ISRAELI AMERICANS

When explaining why the land is so important to both groups and why it is worth fighting for—thus justifying group involvement in the conflict—individuals I interviewed relied upon often-told stories about the history of the territory and their peoples' place in it. First generation Israelis frequently mentioned how the history of the Jewish people and Zionism were heavily-discussed topics throughout their youth. "Efrat"—a forty-four year old woman from whom I gathered a life history—grew up mostly in Israel, all the way through her military service, after which time she moved with her husband to the United States to attend college. She recalls being raised with a strong sense of Zionism in Israeli schools, and was even encouraged as a teenager to dress androgynously so as to appear "like a Zionist pioneer."

"Maytal" is thirty-eight and married with four children, two born in Israel and two in the U.S. She has lived in both the United States and Israel since birth. She was in Israel all through high school, did her mandatory military service, and attended college there. Having been in North Carolina as a post-doctoral student for the past five years, she and her husband are currently trying to decide where in the world to begin their careers. As a parent, Maytal is worried about the safety of her family should they choose to live in Israel, but she feels culturally isolated and lonely in the United States: "Really, I feel I have the choice between living without a soul and being alone and being kind of miserable but knowing my family is safe, or living with a soul but all the rest is gone." She remains connected to the conflict in Israel because "...what happens there is part of me."

Maytal learned throughout her schooling that Jews have always been hated wherever they go, and based on her reception of anti-Semitic comments from her coworkers here, she is not sure that has changed very much. Living in Israel she never felt different because everyone around her was the same, but here she feels pressure to represent Jews and Israelis well so people will not think badly of them. Sometimes she wishes that she were not a part of this group, so she would not have to carry the burden of historical persecution and the conflict with her wherever she goes.

"Noam," a sixty-four year old immunologist with three grown boys, has lived in America since he finished his PhD almost forty years ago. He was raised in Israel by Revisionist Zionists[1] who fought fiercely for Israeli independence in 1948. Over time he has become "…even more convinced that that's the right direction," based on what he sees as a "lack of true commitment to peace by the Arabs."

Mainly drawing upon the Holocaust, several Jewish Israeli members of both generations explained how they feel that the continuing existence of Israel is crucial for Jews' survival. Anxieties amongst the Jewish diaspora give rise to what has been called the "just in case" syndrome, where Israel is perceived as a safe haven in case of an upsurge in anti-Semitism; this perception is a primary way that Israel factors into Jewish diaspora identity (Ben-Moshe, 2007). First generation Israelis commonly articulated memories of feeling safe and protected as Jews only within Israel. Collective stories about ancestral heritage, such as the Holocaust and the global history of anti-Semitism, help reinforce group solidarity and ethnic identity, and the more often the stories are told and retold, the stronger the sense of unification with the group becomes (Patterson, 2006). Therefore, continuing to remember the Holocaust, as is encouraged by the popular Jewish phrase "never forget," helps one maintain a sense of group loyalty and

---

[1] Revisionist Zionism was created by Ze'ev Jabotinsky, who promoted a "revision" of the "practical Zionism" developed by David Ben Gurion. While the latter focused on founding the independent nation of Israel, the former emphasized "political Zionism." Jabotinsky led a movement aimed at garnering British aid to Jews in settling the land during the early Revisionist period. Later on, Revisionist groups working independently of Jabotinsky implemented violent tactics to drive the British authorities out of Palestine so that the Jewish state could be established (Kaplan, 2005).

camaraderie in the face of perceived outsider rejection from anti-Semitic populations. As Keightley (2010) has discussed, discursive constructs such as clichés (e.g., "never forget"), have the potential to mediate individuals' personal narratives. Several subjects spoke about the historical and ongoing persecution of Jews and connected it to their sense of self and group allegiances.

"Liat" is a thirty-year-old woman who lived in the United States from age seven through eighteen but otherwise lived her life in Israel. She moved back to the U.S. the fall before our interview to obtain her PhD and was pregnant with her and her husband's first child. For her, Israel is the only safe place in the world for Jews, because it is their sole real home. As she puts it, "…like Israel's your homeland, it's like your mother and father—they'll accept you whatever happens to you… everyone else will be anti-Semitic, just like they were." Israel's existence makes her feel safe, even in the United States, and she plans to go back one day. This sentiment expresses both a diasporic connection to the ethnic group worldwide, and the maintenance of ties to the homeland despite migration.

"Rachel" is thirty-nine, working on a PhD, and has lived in the U.S. for the past twelve years. Her two children and husband live with her. She connects a history of Jewish persecution to why the conflict is a necessary evil—in order to secure a safe Jewish homeland: "…I'm sure there's a huge effect of everything the Jews have been through, especially the Holocaust, to everything that's going on in Israel right now." She also noted how she was shocked by the racism directed at her here (she has been lumped by Americans into one racial category—Mediterranean—which includes anyone of Arab or Middle Eastern descent, and to her this is racist) because it never happened in Israel, where she was usually only surrounded by other Jews.

"Moshe" is a forty-two year old stay-at-home father of two who moved to the U.S. when he was twenty-four. He expressed more direct frustration with the Arab nations surrounding Israel who he says will not let Israel live in peace, and he linked this current violence to historical precedents:

> I mean, Jews never have an easy life in history. Everybody was against Jewish people, no matter what. Finally we made a country, a state for the Israeli, and still we have conflicts with Arabs around it. I mean, this had to be a Jewish state, in Israel, and instead of letting us live in peace, all of the Arabs

> around us decided to go against us and destroy us. I don't know why.

Moshe's storytelling works to reinforce the commonly-shared group ideology that positions Israelis as perpetual victims surrounded by numerous larger Arab nations who want to annihilate them. His articulations help validate canons of conflict theory by showing how conflict between groups creates perceived divisions—an "us versus them" mentality—and it also helps keep the diaspora united.

Other respondents pushed this notion farther by recalling the more widespread, media-derived notion that Jews and Arabs have been fighting for thousands of years, and thus cannot and will not ever get along (Ackerman, 2001; Kamalipour, 1997). "Ofer," a restaurateur and father of three children, who grew up on a kibbutz in Israel and moved here eighteen years ago, articulates this collectively-shared myth:

> I mean, enough is enough. You're going to kill my side, we kill your side. This started in the Bible, but generations change, things change, so maybe let's sit down and come to a conclusion and really have peace that everybody will be happy and everybody will live with each other . . . I mean we had this for years. If you look in the bible this is where Amalek is; it's always an area with trouble, long, long ago.

"Tzipora" is a forty year old mother of two who was raised in Israel, lived throughout South America, and moved to the United States nine years ago. She is so passionate about the conflict and Israel's need to exist that she works for a national organization promoting relations between Jews in Israel and America. Tzipora sees living in Israel again as a strong possibility because she views few places as safe for Jews, having experienced anti-Semitism in South America (such as the 1994 bombing of a Jewish center in Buenos Aires). She linked the conflict to her past: "I have family who died in the Holocaust. I have family who built Israel…and I have another cousin who was killed in the War of Yom Kippur." Again, here we see the pattern of shared legends of persecution—past and present—working to tie group members to a common heritage and group identity, despite their removal from the conflict site.

Because of Jews' historical experiences with persecution and prejudice, Maytal feels an obligation to move back and fight for Israel to remain the one safe place for Jews worldwide. She also worries that one day Jews may no longer be welcome in the United States. Asked what about the conflict makes it important to her even though she no longer lives in Israel, she responded:

> Well it's my country, it's my homeland, it's my people, it's my history. You know I feel like there's a big burden on my shoulders, and not just here, you know in this world, to live and that's it. Because all my grandparents had to come to Israel from a very wealthy and good life in Europe and they had no choice. They had to leave everything and come to Israel. My grandmother was even fifteen when she came to Israel, she had to build her whole life and never saw her family again. All this came for some reason. I feel like I can't totally disregard that and say, well that's their problem, they built that country for them, and I want a better life in the States. It haunts me all the time. I think one day somebody might come here and tell me that Jews are no longer wanted. So I feel a big responsibility to go back and maintain Israel . . . It's an immediate worry and also kind of a historical view of worry, knowing that there's a reason for that country.

Both Tzipora and Liat claim that distancing themselves from the conflict has allowed them to see that Israel must do whatever it needs to in order to survive, and they feel less critical of Israel's actions now than they did while living in Israel.

"Gil" is a twenty-seven year old who always lived in Israel until he came to North Carolina for graduate school almost four years ago. He describes himself as someone who hates "…the whole group thing, as I call it. Like creating these artificial divisions between…like making unbreachable divisions based on nation, ethnicity, race, gender sometimes…" He feels connected to the conflict because all of his family and friends are in Israel, because he thinks Israel "has its own unique culture which…is worthwhile of continuing in existence," and because he always wants to have a place to escape to if necessary, although he currently does not plan on ever moving back. He, like Noam and several others, says, "I think it's important to have at least one state for that nationality, partly because of historical persecutions against Jews."

In all of these examples, we observe how collectively-held memories of the Holocaust and Jewish persecution are used by first generation Jewish Israelis to defend their need for a homeland, and thus their involvement in the conflict over land. Stories and history work bidirectionally; each shapes the other as we selectively reinterpret reality in terms of the past (Fivush, 2008). Several scholars (Keightley, 2010; Misztal, 2010; Olick, 1999; Ram, 2009; Yerushalmi, 1982) have discussed how collective memories are drastically selective; certain memories live on while the rest are discarded, and the collective memory acquires a mythical component. In such a way, the history of ethno-religious persecution is used by Jewish Israeli subjects as grounds for the necessity of Israel. Social memory has been discussed by Burke (1989) as "a convenient piece of shorthand which sums up the rather complex process of selection of interpretation" (as cited in Olick & Robbins, 1998, p. 110). Historical factors, such as the overall successful integration of Jews in America over time (Brodkin, 1998; Gold, 1997, 2007), are deemphasized in favor of those persecution-themed experiences such as the Jewish ghettos in Europe and the Holocaust, which all work to convince the audience of the need for a safe place belonging to the Jewish people.

SECOND GENERATION JEWISH ISRAELI AMERICANS

"David" is a thirty-four year old dentist who visited Israel frequently as a child but has not been there since 2000 and does not plan to return. He connects the conflict to historical conditions because "...God, there's so little land that's available there and it's the only place where I guess Jews consider themselves having a homeland . . . I hate to see them lose more land, you know?" "Sasha" is twenty-five and works in the high tech field. She has lived most of her life in the United States—her mother moved her to Israel from age fourteen to eighteen, at which point she returned to the U.S. Both her mother and younger sister remain in Israel. Describing a collective memory we heard similarly articulated by Moshe and David, Sasha mentions "...You look at Israel's history and it's always been one of the little guy trying to fight off all the big, bad Arab countries around it. So it's kind of like, yeah, root for the underdog." David and Sasha do not directly mention the history of persecution in their explanation of the need for a Jewish homeland; they allude to the history of the conflict more in terms of Arab-Israeli discord.

"Shai" is a twenty-six year old graduate student who grew up in Israel, England, Hong Kong, and Botswana, and moved to the United States when he was twenty-three. He identifies himself as a second generation Israeli. Shai volunteers in the West Bank every summer to promote peace in that region. He ties his volunteerism to the way he sees himself—"So my identity is very much tied with activism, and my activism is very much tied with Israel and Palestine work. So it's very much shaped my identity." What is interesting in his case is that he does link the history of Jewish persecution to the existence of Israel, but instead of seeing it as justification for involvement in the conflict, he sees it as an ironic shift where Israelis (and thus Jews) moved from "the state of being oppressed to being oppressors." Efrat shares this outlook: "Zionism has come to mean occupied, you know, people who have been occupying a piece of land for almost forty years now." This comparative perspective between what Jews historically endured and their current relationship with Palestinians was a common theme among the Palestinian Americans that I interviewed, and will be discussed later in this chapter.

In congruence with claims by Hobsbawm (1972), Shai and Efrat demonstrate that being a member of any community and having a group-related identity involves situating oneself in light of the community's past, even if only by rejecting it. Shai believes that the Jewish population of Israel, with its greater access to money and power (largely funded by the United States in the form of economic and military aid), is now directing toward the Palestinians the same kind of discriminatory actions historically brought against Jews. He expresses this viewpoint with the following:

> And there was a wonderful line from poetry, I can't remember exactly, but an Arab Jew was in conversation with a European Jew and the European Jew asks, "Who are you?" and the Arab Jew replies, "I am an Arab Jew", and the European Jew asks, "How can you say that when they want to kill us all?" and so the Arab Jew says, "How can you say you're a European Jew when they already have?"

Tamar Katriel (2009) has written about Israeli soldier activists who used personal war narratives to question the morality behind the occupation. In parallel fashion, Shai and Efrat's perceptions of their group's actions function as counter-memories challenging dominant discourses. Such narratives are powerful in that they directly challenge the common assumptions of their fellow group members.

"Leah" is thirty, married without children, and in medical school. She visited Israel every few years during her childhood but had not been back for six years. Like the first generation Jewish Israelis, she referenced the collectively-shared historical memory of the ongoing need for a Jewish nation:

> *Leah*: I mean, there's kind of an undertone driven home to any Jewish person, and the Jewish education of—Jewish people were persecuted throughout history and this is just another example of that persecution. So it taints how Jewish people view this conflict. It doesn't help when the Iranian president says "We'd like to wipe Israel off the map."
>
> *Interviewer*: And you personally feel that's affected your relationship [to the conflict] as well, having that historical precedent?
>
> *Leah*: Sure, yeah. I mean, I'm not thinking, oh, the Arabs are the same thing as the Nazis. I mean, I don't think that's the same thing, but it's like, I mean there's like a historical background that is kind of reinforced over and over in Jewish education and holidays and stuff like that. I'm sure it affects the way that I view the conflict in Israel right now.

She later discussed how her opinions on the conflict were shaped by her parents' views and experiences there. Her father has told her how he had Arab friends as a child, but the ongoing conflict has deepened the divide and made those types of relationships rare. This type of testimony was frequently cited—nostalgia for a time when Jews and Arabs lived in relatively peaceful coexistence in the region. It stands in opposition to narratives such as Ofer's about millennia-long conflict, and it is powerful in that it convinces the audience that peace was once there and could conceivably exist again.

While both of these collective myths—the one about a time of peace, the other about a long history of violence—are based on oversimplifications and distortions of the past, they are powerful and contradictory tools that work to either create hope for an end to the conflict or fear that it will never cease, depending on one's outlook. They also work to keep group members attached to the diasporic community and to their ethnic identity. These dichotomous outlooks on the future can be held simultaneously by one person, depending on her or his stage in life or the current state of the conflict. For example, as I will discuss later on, several interviewees described how they felt optimistic during the peace process in the early 1990s, and then were even more disappointed once it fell apart after the assassination of Prime Minister Yitzhak Rabin in 1995. Memory, and the selective process of recollection, is not a static thing carried from the past to the present, but is instead a fluctuating process that works differently over time (Keightley, 2010; Zelizer, 1995). Bruner (1990) and Calhoun (1994) have warned us against essentializing identities; instead, we should regard them as undergoing a continual process of construction in narrative form.

Halbwachs (1992) and Zerubavel (1996) noted that collective memories can be self-incorporated even when they were not part of a direct experience; this explains how second generation individuals can have their identities shaped by homeland stories without ever having lived in the homeland. As we discern from research on how stories are shared and learned, and also from my respondents' own words, second generation Jewish Israelis (like Leah and many others) learned how to reconstruct the past from their parents who lived in Israel (Ben-Ze'ev, 2005; Hammer, 2005; Fivush, 2008; Orbuch, 1997). Misztal (2010) identified collective memories as a "chain of transmissions" (p. 29) across generations. Meanwhile, Schwartz's (1996) social memory metaphor of a lamp—illuminating what is involved in belonging to a group—is useful for understanding how Israeli parents impart upon their children the importance of remembering the reasons for Israel's creation and the necessity of its continuing existence.

FIRST GENERATION PALESTINIAN AMERICANS

Religious stories about the history of the land and people were frequently mentioned in the interviews, but in unexpected ways. Despite the presence of many religious individuals in my sample,

Jewish Israeli American subjects rarely alluded to Israel being ordained as the Jewish homeland by God, as written in the Old Testament. I found this interesting, since it is often claimed that Jewish identity and the symbolic importance of Israel to Jews worldwide, especially religious Jews, is intimately tied to these theological territorial claims (Davies, 1982). It was actually the Palestinian American subjects who frequently mentioned this Jewish tenet as a reason why the Israelis feel a sense of ownership over the land. These subjects also frequently used Islamic principles to frame their historically-related stories of conflict.

I conducted a life history with Hassan, a forty-four year old father of three who was forced out of Gaza in his youth, fled to Kuwait as a refugee, and moved to the United States after high school to obtain a college education. Hassan, a Muslim, sees everything in terms of Islam, which he says is centered on peace and coexistence. In contrast to the common perception that Jews and Arabs have always been fighting, he recalled a history of Jews and Arabs living and working together. His views are substantiated by Marvasti and McKinney (2004), who articulated that the Koran preaches peace and that the history of Muslim rule reveals they were exceptionally tolerant of Christians and Jews, allowing them to practice their respective religions freely. Hassan alleges that those who deny this past are those who benefit from the continuation of the conflict:

> And even the prophet Muhammad, the first thing, when he starts spreading the religion of Islam, he was telling the people, his followers, to make sure to give the people of the book—the Christians and the Jews—a safe haven. You protect them, you protect their holy places, you protect their identities, no ethnic cleansing, because they could've done it if they were savages back then when they had the power. They could've ethnically cleansed everybody non-Muslim. But that never happened. They left the identity of the Jews, they left the identity of the Christians, and they created harmonic coexistence . . . They got safe havens among the Muslims when they were escaping from the persecution in Europe. When they were persecuted in Europe, they were coming to the Middle East and living with the Muslims. So don't tell me now the Jews and the Arabs hate each other and they cannot live, and therefore we have to create a separated… we have to

> put a wall between them. Those people who preach that kind of thinking are the, the people who support segregation, people who support prejudice, and people who support superiority of one race over another race. And here we go back to Hitler's stance.

Hassan mentioned the history of Jewish persecution as a reason why Jews had to flee Europe and come to Israel. While he invokes a story similar to those told by the Jewish Israelis, his explanation for how it has influenced the land's inhabitants turns from one about safety and protection to one of unquestioned colonization and persecution. A common theme discussed both in scholarly literature (Ellis, 2009; Gur-Ze'ev & Pappé, 2003; Said, 1979) and these interviews is the perception of parallels between persecution of Jews in Europe and the following persecution of Palestinians by members of that very population. In reference to what he calls the "subhuman element" of the treatment of Palestinians, Hassan says,

> And the Jews went through that in Germany. That's what kinda really makes me wonder, I mean. I mean, especially with the Israelis, I mean a lot of the population living in Israel who came from Europe who went through this, who had seen the Holocaust.

A commonly-held collective memory in Jewish history speaks of pioneering Jews venturing into a barren and empty desert in Palestine and making the land and life there flourish (Gerber, 2003; Peled, 1992). A crucial element left out of this tale is the presence of thousands of Arabs living in towns and villages there for hundreds of years. If Palestinians are included in the Israeli version of this story at all, a "flight and abandonment" narrative is used to explain how and why they left (Ram, 2009). The dominant Zionist narrative emphasizes refugee responsibility for the mass exodus and frames Jewish military actions solely in political terms (Nets-Zehngut, 2008). Many scholars (Fivush, 2008; Keightley, 2010; Misztal, 2010; Olick, 1999; Ram, 2009) have theorized about this process of filtering history in the creation of collective memories. Keightley (2010) claims that as individuals and groups construct memories and identities, memories deemed socially unacceptable are omitted. Misztal's (2010) "social forgetting" and Ram's (2009) "narrated forgetting" both refer to this practice of creating and sharing a historical narrative that recalls certain details while disregarding others.

Ram (2009) has referred to Israel's omission of the nakba (specifically events like looting of possessions, expulsion from homes, and killing of prisoners) in their collective memory as "active disremembering," but for the Palestinians I interviewed, these elements of the past play crucial roles in the current conflict. The Palestinians collectively remember generations of their families living on the land, and see the inception of the State of Israel as a cataclysmic interruption in this history which changed Palestinians' lives forever. With the creation of a safe homeland for Jews escaping the Holocaust came the usurpation of Palestinian land and forced exile of their people.

"Gameel" is a forty-three year old father of two. He grew up in Jerusalem before his family was ejected during the Six-Day War in 1967. He sees the previously-mentioned historical precedents of the Holocaust and the following Palestinian occupation as the foundation of the conflict there today:

> It's so sad really—of course they're terrified with everything that's going on in Europe after World War II, and they're told, look, there's this place you can go where there are no people. It's that whole land-without-people myth. So they sell everything, they go and they're all excited, and they show up and they're like, oh, there are people here. Well, what do you do at that stage? Now that is a tragedy. It's like, what a sad situation because now it sets up a conflict right there for political purposes for somebody else's desire.

"Mansur" is fifty-five and married with three children. He moved to America thirty years ago with a PhD and works in the health research field. He too expressed this collective memory of Palestinian history:

> I mean, the fact that the Jews came from persecution—that earned them tremendous sympathy. And unfortunately the world in this arena, where they were trying to sort of compete with who is giving to the Jewish people after the suffering they had in Europe over the years, so there were a lot of people in countries trying to sort of make up for it. So essentially in that rush to make it up for them and sympathize,

> they looked the other way from what they are doing to the Palestinians, to the local inhabitants of the land, to the natives of the land, if you will.

"Safia" is married with three daughters and is in her late thirties. She grew up in Palestine and moved to the United States at age seventeen. Like the others, she linked her views on the conflict to these historical circumstances; however, in congruence with Bruner (1990) and Calhoun (1994), who see the identity process as continuous and shaped by changing narratives, she is able to acknowledge shifts in her perspective over time:

> Even viewing the Holocaust, growing up there [in Israel/Palestine] was completely different than viewing it here [in the U.S.]. Over there it's like, it's the excuse to take our country and kick us all out. Okay, the Holocaust was terrible, but why is it the justification for what's happening to us? You don't feel the pain that's going on behind it until again here in the United States you talk to the Jewish friends.

For Safia, interacting with the Other, even though it was away from the conflict site, was crucial in evoking her compassion and changing her perceptions of the opposing group. As she put it, "The expression is: an enemy is someone whose story we have not heard."

Like Hassan, Safia recalls the collective story of how Jews and Arabs historically coexisted in the land, and contrasts that with the Jews' experiences in Europe:

> As a minority you always complain, but Jews in Arab countries for centuries have prospered—they are affluent, they're educated, they have good positions. Okay, the religion of the land is not their religion, so you feel sensitive about that. But they were part of the countries and they were never massacred. There was no Holocaust; there was no putting them in ghettos. They were part of society. They didn't have ghettos in the Arab countries.

Thus, several first generation Palestinians interviewed invoked the Holocaust and other historical persecution of Jews in the process of questioning how Israelis cannot see what are, in their eyes, glaring parallels between the Holocaust and the Palestinian occupation.

SECOND GENERATION PALESTINIAN AMERICANS

Thirty-seven year old "Ahmed" was raised in Jordan and moved to America twelve years ago. He owns two restaurants with his brothers. Like some of the first generation Palestinian Americans, he refutes the notion that Jews and Arabs have always been fighting, and thinks these stories only work to perpetuate the conflict and dampen hope for its cessation:

> *Interviewer*: Do you think there's any connection between your opinions and reactions to the conflict and the history of your people?
>
> *Ahmed*: No, the history has nothing to do with my reaction. The conflict is sixty years old, it's not 2,000 years old. That's my answer right away—oh you guys have been fighting… it's sixty years old! Before that there was nothing called Palestinians or Israelis; before that there were Jews, Christians, and Muslims that lived under different occupation—either Roman or Greek or Crusades or whatever. They were all occupied; they were all together part of the same thing. Prior to that, yes, you have Babylon but that was 2,000 years ago. You cannot put that with the current day; it has nothing to do with it.

Ahmed's opinions on the Israeli explanation of the Holocaust as justification for their claim to the land are congruent with first generation Palestinian Americans':

> And that's why I don't like the Israeli approach which says that the majority of Israelis are Ashkenazi so they lived a bad time in Europe, they know what it means to be picked and tortured. And then I'm looking and it's like, for God's sake, I mean you're not doing as bad, but come on! It's almost as bad! I mean you're driving them to kill themselves.

"Yasir" is forty-five, works at a family-owned restaurant, and is married with four children. He was born in Palestine but then fled to Kuwait, where he lived until he moved to the United States at age nineteen. Like Ahmed, he finds it hard to accept how the Jews had an even worse experience in Europe, and now are doing to the Palestinians what was done to them. He expressed a desire that I heard from most of the interviewees: he thinks "…it could easily be peaceful if they just give us a land and get out of our… not give us all our land… okay, until the '67 [land divisions] and stay out of that area—nothing would happen."

"Naimah" is presently in college after spending most of her youth in Kuwait. She confessed that her views are not yet clearly defined, as she is only nineteen and does not yet know have a well-established sense of identity. When asked about her ethnic identity she said:

> …well, I mean, when I think about who I am, I don't even have an answer. I don't even know am I Palestinian, am I American? I'm like, in between. I don't have a place. I can't really find a place.

One thing she is clear about is that she does not like organized religion, because she sees how people (she gives the example of Zionists) use it to justify their mistreatment of others. The main differences between Israelis and Palestinians for her are related to religion and history:

> I guess the major difference is the whole religious aspect. They [Jewish Israelis] believe in their right to the land, God gave them that land. But the Arabs, the Palestinians, they feel that they were there and just got kicked out. It just wasn't fair.

"Raya" is twenty and an undergraduate. She identifies as Muslim and wears a *hijab*. Like Naimah, she feels that religion is all too often used to legitimize land rights at the expense of other groups.

"Asim" is a forty-three year old father of four and an entrepreneur; born in Kuwait to Palestinian parents who were exiled by the occupation, he has now lived in the United States for twenty-seven years. Asim, like Hassan and also Yasir, consistently drew connections between Islam and his actions and viewpoints. His religion serves as a bridge between himself and his life in the United States and Palestine because, "It's truly a land of peace. It's a holy area." "Burhan," forty-seven, married with six children, and owner of a local Middle Eastern restaurant chain, grew up in Kuwait and Lebanon and moved here twenty-nine years ago. He too claims that Islam is the basis for how he views the conflict: "...If people understood that the more people are educated in their faith, the more peaceful they will become, it would change a whole lot."

In Islam, home is not geographically fixed but is wherever one currently is located (Huttunen, 2005). Burhan, Asim, and several other self-identified Muslims mentioned that because of their religion they do not believe in country borders or ownership of land. They think that these are modern notions created by man as a way to control and dominate others, and for them this applies directly to the Israeli occupation of the land. All of the divisions between the colonizer and the colonized create further suffering and fuel the continuing conflict.

CONCLUSIONS

Just as with Israeli Americans, collective memories and common stories, including religious ones, are used by members of both Palestinian generations to explain their views on the historical foundations of the conflict. The same story of the creation of Israel in 1948 takes on two very different meanings, depending on which side of the conflict one falls. It is either a story of final redemption or the beginning of oppression and exile. And like their second generation Israeli American counterparts, second generation Palestinians have been raised by their families to be aware of and emotionally connected to their people's suffering in the homeland. Here again we see that via parent-child socialization processes, memories and perceptions of the conflict can shape how individuals see themselves, despite their not having experienced the conflict directly.

For both ethnic groups involved in the conflict, collective memories help them maintain their group bonds across physical space and identity continuity. As MacIntyre (2007) acknowledged, historical identity and social identity go hand in hand and belonging entails aligning oneself with the group's past—though sometimes by rejecting that past. However, we will see in the next chapter how conflict-related identity effects derive from more than group-level narratives and historical antecedents; a central tool used by both generations is the recollection of memories and accounts of immediate experiences with the Palestinian-Israeli conflict.

CHAPTER 2:

Stories about Homeland Conflict

The land dispute between Palestinians and Jewish Israelis has undeniably created group-level divides and antagonism which transcend the conflict site. In this chapter, I explore how my subjects use either their own accounts of homeland conflict or their parents' shared memories to draw connections between their current diasporic lives, ethnic identities, and the ongoing conflict back home. In *Racism without Racists* (2003), Eduardo Bonilla-Silva claims that stories transcend the level of individual interaction and work to determine the social structure by reinforcing the status quo (Bonilla-Silva, 2003, p. 75). Stories are seen as both social products and ideological social tools; they represent consensus, which makes them seem factual, and their repetition augments the collective's shared social perceptions (Bonilla-Silva, 2003, p. 76). Applying this perspective to tenets of conflict and transnationalism theories, I use my interview-based data to examine how subjects use these recollections to reinforce notions of "us versus them" and victim versus oppressor.

As discussed earlier, extensive research on transnational ties has shown that migrant families orient particular, meaningful aspects of their lives around their country of origin. When asked in the interview about homeland issues that are important to her or him as a Palestinian American or Jewish Israeli American living in the United States today, every person with whom I spoke, except one, said that their main concern was the conflict between Israel and either the Palestinians specifically or the surrounding Arab nations more broadly. The common sentiment among both groups is that the conflict's history pervades the lives of group members anywhere they live, and continuously shapes their identities. In this way, they come to view homeland issues as transnational platforms of concern. Through the process of caring about and supporting the end of the conflict there, they are encouraged to continue identifying with and acting on behalf of the country of origin.

As I demonstrate through my findings, the details of this process are different for each person; it is not a uniform or a linear progression. A person can be strongly attached to both home and host country simultaneously and in varying ways (Gans, 2007; Levitt & Waters, 2002; Portes & Rumbaut, 2006; Wald, 2009; Waters & Ueda, 2007; Zimmermann et al., 2007). While I look for general trends and patterns in diasporic connections to conflict, I also pay significant attention in the following analyses to multiplicity in these transnational connections. Both first and second generation Jewish Israelis and Palestinians relied upon a combination of testimonials (stories that directly involve them or people close to them) and more generalized stories/collective memories to articulate for both themselves and the audience what role homeland conflict plays in their social world and self-concept. The main recurring narratives brought up in discussions of homeland experiences with conflict involved wartime occurrences and episodes of violence; other types of encounters with members of the other group; for Israelis, military service; and for Palestinians, loss of home and forced expulsion.

Before I discuss respondents' experiences with conflict, it is important and relevant to mention here an interesting viewpoint often expressed by only the Jewish Israeli subjects. In contrast to mainstream, often media-derived characterizations which portray Israel and the occupied territories as dangerous areas where one's life is threatened daily, those who have been there express the notion of "life goes on." Although every Jewish Israeli interviewed acknowledged that the conflict over land is the most crucial issue, they also noted that people in Israel continue to lead normal lives there. Tzipora, who moved to the United States from Israel nine years ago, used a testimonial to explain how being in the homeland makes all the difference for understanding this key distinction:

> Well, it's interesting—I took my kids for the first time to Israel last year, and they were very afraid, especially my daughter. She said, my friends are going to Hawaii and you're

> taking me to the war, because we went in the middle of the war a little bit. And I was like, you will feel safe there. She has completely different expectation from what she got. She said that because of CNN because actually that's the way that they most get informed—TV . . . It's completely distorted and they will show the worst because that's what will bring the audience . . . So they got to a country where they saw something completely different. They saw young soldiers who hate going to war, who are good people, who are concerned if they need to aim at someone. She saw kids walking in the street by themselves in a different society. Here I don't let her go by herself to get an ice cream. There it was 10:30 at night and she went with a friend to get an ice cream, because the streets were full of kids, and so it was different. They had different expectations. They didn't know what Israel is because they got it from the TV.

Moshe, a stay-at-home father who grew up in Israel, brought up this idea repeatedly throughout his interview with multiple testimonials.

> Some people are like, I can't live over there; you never know what's going to happen. [But] people live over there. They go out. I go to Israel, I go dancing. During the war—I went last summer, I went Israeli folk dancing every night in Tel Aviv. I live! So there is war in the north, I know don't go to the north . . . So it's scary to live there, but you know, it's part of life. One thing about that, if you're going to be dead, you're going to be dead no matter where you are. It's a part of life.

"Zev" has lived in Spain, France, Israel, and is attending college in the United States. Speaking about his teenage years in Israel, he said, "And then sometimes the Israeli army would say, 'Hey, there's a guy [a potential terrorist] who managed to get into central Israel,' and so we wouldn't go out that weekend." He later added, "I feel worse living in

Paris than in Israel. In Israel I know that I'm being protected by someone…"[1]

Leah, another second generation Israeli American, made a similar statement about daily life and conflict there:

> For example, the Arab-Israeli conflict, I guess that could be a barrier to going to visit, but we're going anyways and my parents have gone when things were more active than they are now, and it's kind of like, your life must go on.

She later noted that these opinions of hers reflect those of her parents, who grew up there, supporting claims that family is the crucial link for learning how to belong to a group through the use of collective memories (Hammer, 2005; Mistzal, 2010). Sasha, who lived in Israel during her teenage years as well, told me how she does not recall talking about the conflict at all while she lived there because "…we were just clueless high school kids just trying to be normal and trying to get on with life." "Dalia," a nineteen year old college student whose mother is Israeli, clarified the difference between seeing the conflict from afar and living it on a daily basis: "But like my relatives, they're so used to everything there that it's like, normal. So it doesn't bother them. So, like, I think we're bothered by everything more than they are."

It seems that for second generation Israelis, either hearing about the homeland from one's parents or being there and verifying that indeed the conflict does not pervade every aspect of daily life helps them understand the complex and somewhat contradictory notion that although the conflict is the central group issue, it does not stop people from going about their everyday lives. This common perspective was notably absent among the Palestinian American subjects.

As opposed to the Israelis who talked about the experience of negotiating a normal life around the conflict, the Palestinians with whom I spoke all described a quite different reality for people living in the homeland. Perhaps the best way to appreciate these very divergent group-level experiences is to frame them in terms of power—the experiences of colonizer and colonized. The colonizer exerts control

---

[1] Post-World War II, France's unitary ethnic system caused Jewish affiliation with Zionism to be culturally taboo, and this hostility towards Zionists is claimed by some to have persisted over time (Waldinger & Fitzgerald, 2004).

over the colonized people's personal freedoms and rights, and has the capacity to monopolize valued resources such as land, education, and economic opportunity (Memmi, 1965). As I will show in the following section, which explores narratives about conflict and violence in the homeland, Palestinian Americans describe collective memories about daily life quite differently from their Jewish Israeli American counterparts. Power relations shape the connections that transnational immigrants have with both sending and receiving countries, and their divergent experiences with conflict have differential effects on Palestinian and Jewish Israeli American identity.

FIRST GENERATION PALESTINIAN AMERICANS

Hassan had his entire life trajectory altered by war. He was born in Gaza and at age five, while his family was temporarily in Kuwait, the '67 War occurred and his family was not allowed to return home. From that point on he lived as a refugee with very limited rights in Kuwait, and his only continuing association with Gaza—a place where his family had lived for seven hundred years—was when the Israeli authorities would "grant us a visa, like a visitor" and allow his family to come back for a couple of months every summer. Hassan recalled memories from these visits, from age six to seventeen, of humiliating strip searches he was forced to undergo each time he passed through the border crossings:

> I mean, they're not harsh but it creates, uh, a sour memory, especially when I was like ten and they ask you to strip and then they don't do anything! They tell you to put your clothes back on…that was psychological. I mean I think, uh… (pauses)… it's kinda trying to make people feel not very welcome.

This memory of border patrol harassment turned out to be a very common theme.

When he reached adulthood, traveling to and within Palestine became even more difficult for Hassan. What used to be a forty-five minute trip from the Tel Aviv airport to his home now took seven hours because he was no longer allowed to fly into Israel and was forced to go through Cairo instead. The Gaza of his childhood transformed from a beautiful place to an overpopulated territory after the Palestinians were displaced in 1948:

> So all the sudden the population of Gaza quadrupled within a short period of time, from, you're talking about from fifty thousand within fifteen years became almost a million and a half. Yeah, all refugee camps, living under poverty, have nothing.

He described the refugee camps:

> *Hassan*: I mean, Tijuana, Mexico looks like a beach resort compared to this. I am talking about there is no infrastructure. Sewers running in the streets, poverty . . . The alleys, people made, houses made out of mud and shingles. I mean, literally it's not a life.
>
> *Interviewer*: And there are a lot of young people living there.
>
> *Hassan*: Yeah, it's full of a lot of young people and uh, and the, the elderly who are pretty much kinda left, and now they're living in these refugee camps . . . They are trying to make a living, you know, so they send their kids, they don't go make them finish school. They just send them out while they are kids, young, to go out and start working . . . The Arab populations, the work populations—it's like Mexicans here…they were the cheap labor, you know for Israel. And uh, but, I mean all that now…it became like a major problem. And I, every time I go there now I see that sight, and the minute I step out of Gaza into Israel, it's like a completely different world (pause) even though it's just…
>
> *Interviewer*: You mean like the economic state of it?
>
> *Hassan*: Yeah, I mean, even though they are just miles apart, you know, but it's like two different worlds.

Mansur recollected similar tales of how he "used to visit almost every year" but now does so less frequently because of obstacles and Israeli surveillance; he noted, "It used to be easier . . . but they will identify you through their databases and they will figure you are a Palestinian and you will get really harassed. Plus it became so difficult to move around anything in there." He too shared numerous testimonies about sitting at checkpoints for hours just to travel six miles during his visits there, and sees these hardships as a part of who he is. He wishes he could move back there "and benefit the society there, be part-time living there or somehow. Is it going to happen? It does not look good."

Mansur, like Gameel, Asim, and many others, laments the fact that Palestinians in the United States are unable to help with homeland development (when such help could be a significant potential form of aid) due to a "lack of power, lack of international recognition of their suffering, their support . . . Israel made a lot of mistakes too but never paid for any of their mistakes." Sari Hanafi (2005, p. 98) has discussed the unique experiences of Palestinians as being a "partially diasporized people" because they lack a physical space where they can easily meet and connect, unlike other diasporas who have the basic benefits of passports, nationhood, and visitation opportunities. This divergent aspect of Palestinians' diasporic experience, as compared to Jewish Israelis', is one of many that make up a central theme of this book—the effect of power inequalities on diasporic identity and relations with homeland conflict. Based on pertinent literature (Hammer, 2005; Hanafi, 2005; Khalidi, 1997; Noakes & Wilkins, 2002; Portes & Rumbaut, 2006; Said, 1979), I anticipated and confirmed that Palestinians and Israelis would have differing relations with both the host and home country, as Palestinians have unequal experiences in areas such as the struggle for nationhood and citizenship rights, their fight for outsider legitimization and political representation, international image, experiences with discrimination and stereotyping in the diaspora, and also their involuntary refugee experiences.

Mansur, Hassan, and several others also mentioned their frustration with not being able to return and live in the homes they owned which were taken from them, while meanwhile any Jew in the world can move to Israel and be given immediate citizenship and government aid. Mansur's loss of his family farm has permanently affected him:

> Oh yeah, I mean in my family I lose the farm. My father within weeks died. He could not handle what happened; he just could not do it. I mean a lot of people sympathized with me or sent me an email or card but they have their priorities and their own concerns . . . And I appreciate it but the reality is it's not going to leave the same fingerprints on their lives

> the same way it is on me . . . For me it's an existing issue. Every time I am going to go there I am going to see that farm sitting behind that fence and somebody else is in control of it. So even if I wanted to forget, I would not forget it. The events that is happening, what is going on, is a constant reminder.

Safia echoed the theme of difficulty moving within Palestine with her own stories. She defined homeland conflict in terms of these types of adversities, along with the general lack of human rights and resulting poverty:

> I think the conflict is constant. I mean anything—it's all conflict. As far as people living in the West Bank, it's a conflict every day. Walking or driving or taking a bus from your home to a school and going through several checkpoints and getting beat up or spat at—to me that's a conflict, an ongoing conflict.

Safia used to go back to Israel every three years to renew her paperwork, in order to maintain her Israeli ID for "patriotism reasons, so I can be counted. I didn't want to give up that right, to be counted as a Jerusalem resident." Once she even crossed the bridge from Jordan to Israel, spent the night, and returned to the United States the next morning. But about four years ago she began to think it had become too difficult and dangerous, as she experienced more and more harassment when crossing the border. Ultimately she lost her status as a resident there, but she has not yet given up hope: "I still have a copy of my paper; maybe one day I'll sue and try to get it back."

Like several others, Safia was traumatized by the experience of losing her family home, and tears were streaming down her cheeks, her voice breaking, as she told me the story of how she would occasionally return to visit it. A Jewish family had been given her mother's home and they would let her and her parents in to see it:

> And it's tough; I mean the stuff that they buried in the backyard was dug up and on display everywhere. And my dad was trying to buy them back for her. I think the daughter said no because selling them back to my mom was acknowledging that this was her [Safia's mother's] home…

Sharing such a personal account may serve several important functions, from giving Safia some degree of control and understanding of her situation, to allowing her to cope with an emotional and stressful situation, to hopefully providing some level of closure (Orbuch, 1997). Despite any resolution achieved through the sharing of testimonies, these stories are likely never forgotten and leave an indelible mark on lives and identities.

One way Palestinian respondents described how living through the conflict shapes them is in terms of a burden they always carry. Like the rest of the first generation Palestinians, Safia explained how having family origins and enduring direct conflict in Palestine has permanently affected her:

> *Safia*: ...So I feel like it's a big, big burden. I go through depression phases when things with the conflict get heated. So it's very hard. Psychologically, sometimes I wish could be something else. I want to be from another nationality. I don't want to be a Jew, I don't want to be Palestinian, I don't want to be Indonesian. I want to be somewhere that doesn't have conflict.
>
> *Interviewer*: What is it about these types of conflict that make it important to you even though you no longer live there?
>
> *Safia*: I mean, the fact that I was born and raised there and that my parents have been there for hundreds and hundreds of years, if not thousands of years. It never goes away. It's a part of me. As much as I'm an American citizen—I've lived here longer than I lived there. . . . But you never lose that connection. It's a part of me. It's a part of my parents. You know, you feel sad about bad things happening in Darfur and other places, but it hurts a lot more when it happens back home where I came from, because I lived it. I walked those streets, I know that feeling. I've been stopped at those checkpoints. I've been treated that way. I've seen my brothers get beat up. I've experienced it, so it all is personal to me. And it will always be personal. Even if I never go back to live it will always be personal to me.

The conflict has also shaped the identity of Mansur, and his homeland memories continue to haunt him. The pain it causes him affects his health and productivity. I met with him at his office, and halfway through the interview he pointed out to me a postcard he has up on his wall.

> See that picture of that old man? He's carrying it on his back. This guy is carrying Palestine on his back, it's a burden. That's really my burden. I love this picture. This guy represents me. I am carrying on my shoulders the huge burden of the Palestinian suffering, the pain of the diaspora, being denied the right to be free, to go and visit my family when I want to, to go to the farm that I grew up as a little child around, and to enjoy what my father left me. This is why I'm not a normal person.

He went on to tell me that being a Palestinian motivates him to work harder than everyone else, in order to represent Palestinians in a positive light. He also told me he works longer hours to escape ruminating about the conflict. Had it not been for this burden constantly distracting and consuming him he would "probably be sitting in the White House. I mean, I would probably be a hundred times more productive and successful in my career and my life."

Gameel, who now makes documentaries about the conflict, also informed me that losing the family home was an episode of conflict that continually influences him—hence his career change.

> Well, I've lived through a war there, the '67 War, and my family still lives there. And I know the emotional connection, you know, my family has to the land that they lost and to the home they lost in '48, which is still there…

For him and others who experienced this type of loss, the link to the land includes having family still there, but is mainly focused on having property and homes still there, occupied by others.

> So growing up in this country, if somebody could come in and just push you out of your house and take it, we can't even fathom that…and yet that sort of thing has happened and does happen around the world.

This common heritage and memory joins them all together as a forcibly exiled population. Many of the respondents told me stories about parents or grandparents who still have, and often bring out, the deeds or keys to the house and land they were compelled to leave.

All the Palestinians (and Jewish Israelis) I interviewed who lived in the homeland spoke about how growing up in wartime is something that inevitably and permanently shapes a person. Gameel described what he went through in the '67 Arab-Israeli War and how it influenced him:

> *Gameel*: Well, the thing about conflict, the thing about war that I think most people don't understand, is that it's something that stays with you forever. The notion you go and bomb people for a couple of weeks and then okay, everything is better now, that kind of terrifying experience just doesn't go away. I was about four. I don't remember every detail but things like when a bomb goes off, it's something you feel through your body. And also seeing dead bodies, I mean they're things that you… and the people around you are all scared… I mean, you experience all of that. There are windows shattering, and so I remember a lot of those kinds of things.
>
> *Interviewer*: And at that age it must be even more terrifying because you don't understand.
>
> *Gameel*: Right, but the point being, I think, is that people who go through conflict, it can't help but shape who they are in some way. And for me I think it has caused me to always want to find a solution to conflict, a peaceful kind of way—a dialogue with people, or trying to see what their motivation is, about why it is that they're involved in this conflict. Because I think it's the only way you can bridge that gap. So for me, that's how; it's created somebody who's looking to educate and bridge those gaps of knowledge, or lack of knowledge.

"Umar" is forty-eight, married with four children, and works in real estate. His story is similar to Hassan's in that he was born and raised in Gaza, and then moved temporarily to Kuwait when his father got a two-year teaching contract there. The Gaza Strip was occupied while they were away, and they lost their home and were not allowed to return. He described the experience of having a deed to a home and then having that home stolen, and went on to share a particularly potent memory:

> *Umar*: It affects me when I see my father. I'll tell you a sample example and I'll never, ever in my life forget this sight. We went to visit in 1974 and I was fourteen, fifteen at the time, and I remember it just like I'm looking at you right now. And Mom and Dad, they took us from Gaza Strip, we went through the Israeli border . . . So they went to my dad's hometown at that time, where he was born, and he stood right there and cried his eyes out, because it's like here's where I was born, and we never sold that land. It was taken away from us. That hurts and I'll never forget that sight in my life, as long as I'm alive, because I know I saw my mom and dad both crying, because it was still fresh at that time—we're talking years ago, what thirty-five years ago? And it was fresher then than it is right now. So it touched them and it touched me to watch them with tears coming down their eyes because they lost it.
>
> *Interviewer*: So what kind of emotional reactions do you have to these kinds of events?
>
> *Umar*: Sadness, just sad, it brings a lot of sadness to my heart to see my father suffer so many times, and my family. Maybe I haven't lost anything personally because I never owned a land in my name in Palestine. But mine, my father's… you know that's how people in this country—they hand down what they owned to their children and children and grandchildren. Well, nothing was handed down to me yet.

Here we see that the transmission of ethnic identity as it is related to conflict occurs not just between first and second generation immigrants, but goes back to the relationships of first generation respondents and their parents who experienced dispossession and exile together.

A common link among these first generation Palestinians is that they belong to a cohort that grew up in the 1960s and experienced the loss of their family home during the Six-Day War. As Mannheim

(1952) noted, shared social and political events mold generations through major shared experiences during formative years. These firsthand testimonials are very powerful in evoking an emotional response from the listener—an important distinction between narratives shared by the first generation and those of the second generation. Personalized, descriptive stories and a teller's own emotional response influence the audience in a way that common tales simply cannot (Bonilla-Silva, 2003).

Direct experience with homeland conflict also makes a notable difference for how conflict affects the identities of first versus second generation Palestinian Americans. Echoing central tenets of the previously-cited transnationalism and assimilation literature, Umar described to me how distance and length of time away from the homeland attenuates only certain people's connections to it:

> So as the generations move on, the tie becomes weaker, and the effect on the human being becomes weaker… except the ones that live there. You can't change them, they live it every day. It doesn't get weaker, it actually gets worse.

Mansur explained to me the main differences between himself and his second generation children:

> I am more emotionally attached. I lived in there until the age of eighteen. When that farm was taken away from us, I remember when I was five, six years old that was my dream time to go to the farm and help the family plant citrus trees, and then after hard work we'd have a little picnic lunch on the farm, and then sometimes we'd spend the night on the farm in the spring or the summer, when it's nice. So it's attachment. I'm attached to the land. I mean I know [the kids] sympathize, I know they know about, but it's just no comparison. Actually, one of my concerns is that if something happens to me I'm not sure if they're going to maintain relations with people over there. They really will not have what I have. It's different.

He tells his children that because they lost their real home in Palestine their American residence is a house and not a home, but for them it is the only place they know. It is this key difference—between actually losing one's home and being raised by those who have—that I turn to next in my discussion of second generation Palestinian Americans.

SECOND GENERATION PALESTINIAN AMERICANS

Family is commonly recognized as the primary social institution assisting in the development of ethnic identities among American-born children (Levitt & Waters, 2002; Zhou, 1997; Waters et al., 2010). Among the key mechanisms for this development are language retention (Rebhun & Lev Ari, 2010; Rumbaut, 2002; Waters et al., 2010), parental socialization and control (Kasinitz et al., 2002; Levitt & Jaworsky, 2007; Levitt, 2009; Portes, Fernandez-Kelly, & Haller, 2009; Stepick & Stepick, 2010; Waters et al., 2010), and storytelling (Ben-Ze'ev, 2005; Chamberlain, 2004; Eastmond, 2007; Fivush, 2008; Hammer, 2005; Misztal, 2010; Olick & Robbins; 1998). Additional factors involved in diasporic identity formation of second generation individuals include religious participation (Gold, 2007; Levitt & Jaworsky, 2007; Levitt, 2009; Rumbaut, 2002), homeland information sources (Matar, 2006), visits to the country of origin (when possible) (Gold, 2007), and host country community involvement (Cohen & Gold, 1996; Ellis & Almgren, 2009; Gold, 2007; Gowricharn, 2009; Waters et al., 2010). I will examine in detail how contextual factors—also influenced by parental perspectives—shape the identities of the second generation when I turn to issues of media usage and host country experiences in Chapters Three and Four. In congruence with Haller and Landolt's (2005) assertions, I discovered that the degree to which homeland conflict affects identity is primarily decided by parents and family, who determine the trajectory of transnational ties for their children.

These stories are particularly important for Palestinian Americans as many have never been able to return to the homeland because of visiting restrictions, because they fear the dangers and harassment associated with traveling to and through the area, or because their displacement was such a traumatic ordeal they cannot face returning to the land. It is usually the first reason mentioned that keeps them from visiting their families and showing their children their country of origin. As I will continue to show, this crucial element of having no homeland to claim or return to is a key differentiator for how distant conflict affects the identities of Palestinian Americans versus Jewish Israeli Americans.

Generational status was a consequential mediating factor that emerged from my interviews with second generation Palestinian Americans. Four of the five men I interviewed, whose ages ranged from thirty-seven to forty-eight, had been able to visit Palestine when they were younger and the borders were more accessible. The four women with whom I spoke, whose ages ranged from nineteen to twenty-two, had never been allowed to visit because entering Palestine was seen by their parents as too difficult during their childhood years. There is an alternate possibility that gender may also have played a role here; however, all of the women I interviewed mentioned that their parents wished to take them and their siblings to the homeland but were simply unable to because of access and safety issues. While, therefore, half of the second generation Palestinian subjects have never actually been to Palestine, they all indicated that they see it as their homeland. In comparison, the overwhelming majority of second generation Israelis visited Israel several times throughout their youth—an issue I will discuss towards the end of the chapter.

Ahmed, the thirty-seven year old restaurant owner who grew up as a refugee in Jordan, identifies Palestine as his homeland because his family was there for over eight hundred years. He would like to be able to visit. He has been to the area twice, the last time to give a presentation in Jerusalem (he has a PhD in nutrition from a university in Jordan), and although he did not experience violence while there, he did have a conversation with an Israeli colleague which typified the conflict for him:

> I had known him for years through his writings and he'd known me through my writings. And he goes, like, where are you from? And I looked at him, and I didn't want to smart mouth him in a sense, but I wanted to declare myself, especially since I was inside what I considered Palestine. And I was like, "Well, I'm from a few miles down the road, south of here, and it's a village called Tapasia, but you call it now Yehud." And he goes like, "You're from Yehud?" And I was like, "Yes." He said, "I didn't know there were any Arabs in Yehud." I said, "Well, there wasn't but three women Jews in the village before 1948, and they were married too." And it

> was a little bad comment, well, not bad comment but just an expression of how I felt, and he goes, "Well, yeah, but you're Jordanian born and raised." I said, "No." He goes, "Yeah, your parents immigrated to Jordan, so you're Jordanian." And I didn't even have a chance to answer—my professor's wife was with us, she's from Raleigh, and [to the colleague] she's like, "No . . . you are Dutch because your parents are Dutch, and they chose to immigrate to Canada, so you became Canadian. Now you chose to come here so now you're American. [Ahmed] will always be Palestinian because his parents were kicked out. They did not immigrate." I said [to the wife], "Thank you, well said!" And that's how I feel exactly.

During his only other visit to Palestine, Ahmed remembers being shocked by how small the land was, yet how much of a division existed between the affluent areas of Israel and the ghetto-like refugee camps just miles down the road, where his aunt lived. He told me how he was harassed at checkpoints both in Jerusalem and at the entrance to the refugee camp. He compared the beauty and peace of Jerusalem to the extreme poverty, crowding, and mayhem in the camps, where it was typical to see an "Israeli patrol coming through town, and you see the people running around away from it, they might be shot or something."

Beyond these encounters from his personal experience, Ahmed's conceptions of homeland conflict are formulated around stories told to him as a child by his now-deceased mother and the life lessons that suffering taught her. Her stories were of the same kind collectively shared by first generation respondents:

> She basically left while they were being shot at, you know, the last minute, and she just grabbed her kids and ran away. She even forgot to put her slippers on. And the only thing she had was ten pieces of gold under her head cover, because she was still not married five years and the culture was, after five years she could remove them. So that's how they started their life later on, with these pieces of gold that she had left on her head. As a child growing up without a father, she would start crying and telling me all of these things—"I'm sorry, I should've gotten you a better life but we couldn't. Be tough, be tough, toughen up." And I did.

"Josef," forty-eight and married with two children, works as a psychiatrist. He and one other person in the Palestinian sample deviate from the rest in that they are Greek Orthodox/Christian and not Muslim. He visited Palestine four or five times before age eighteen and then it became too difficult for him to visit. His personalized narratives about homeland conflict are centered on the same topics as the others—border patrol harassment and difficulty moving around the country. According to him, these daily struggles are as important as the more visible, acute conflicts such as Israeli military actions and helicopter attacks:

> There's a conflict at wanting to do your work and having to drive three hours when it used to take ten minutes. Those are what I would call the underlying tension conflicts that are there. You know the car bombings, all that kind of stuff is an overt, aggressive conflict, and the Israeli incursions into those areas with a lot of force and helicopter attacks are just an escalation of what I think is an underlying daily tension conflict.

Josef described the intimidation and questioning by the Israeli Defense Force (IDF) as demeaning and angering—a common characterization from this type of collective memories. Also, just as with Ahmed, Josef's parental stories of conflict had the same themes of forced expulsion and fear of being killed. He told me the following stories, first about his father's and then about his mother's forced retreat from Palestine:

> *Josef*: One day [my father] was going to get on his school bus to go to school. He missed the school bus, and some Jewish settlers blew up that school bus. His mom would not let him go back to school because of that . . . So he went to the American University in Beirut at sixteen, so he grew up in Bethlehem until he was sixteen. My mom grew up in Haifa until she was ten, and then when she was ten, British soldiers came to their house and told them they had to move because they lived on Mt.Carmel, which overlooked the town of Haifa. So they were forced to move to the German Colony, down in Haifa proper, from Mt.Carmel, because there was a concern

among the Jewish settlers that Palestinians on Mt.Carmel would create sniper…

Interviewer: Because they had a lookout up there?

Josef: Yeah. And then when they were down there the '48 war broke out and they were basically run out of their home under gunpoint. So they had to leave.

Interviewer: So they fled to Beirut?

Josef: Uh huh, Beirut. And that's where my mom grew up from the time she was ten until she came to the country to be with my dad.

As a child, Josef, "was kind of antsy about being identified as being an Arab, much less Palestinian," but upon entering college and learning more of the history, "there was a sense of kind of pride in being Palestinian, and I still have that sense of pride of being Palestinian." This later-in-life discovery of pride in nationality proved to be a popular theme among my subjects, and it lends additional credibility to the theorized notion that ethnic identity is not constant across the lifecourse (Bruner, 1990; Calhoun, 1994; Wald, 2009).

Like Ahmed, Josef feels connected to Palestine and the conflict there because "it's where I came from . . . [though] I can't really just freely go back there if I want to." As for how the conflict shapes his identity versus his parents', Josef claimed that they are more connected to it because they lived through it:

Josef: I mean, naturally, my dad will pull out deeds to land he has in Jerusalem. He still has the deeds. We visited my mom's house in Haifa and the person who was renting from them was given the house when they left. And so we were able to talk to him about it, what his memory was of that house. The deed is still in my grandmother's name. So they experienced the loss of what they had.

Interviewer: How do you think that impacts the way they react to it now?

Josef: I mean, it's just the sense again of things were taken away from them. And you know, I think there's still somewhere deep down a hope or a wish that they could get it back, not at someone else's expense, but because it's theirs.

For Josef and the other second generation Palestinians, this is a key distinction between him and his parents: the United States is the only home he knows, and this wish to return does not exist for him in the same way or to the same extent. As part of this desire to return, the first generation also maintains more of their traditional cultural practices, such as language, dress, and lifestyle customs. As Zhou (1997, p. 64) and Portes and Rumbaut (2005) have argued, because they lack the same meaningful ties to the homeland as their parents, second generation immigrants are less likely to consider it as a point of reference, and are instead prone to assess themselves by American standards. These types of discrepancies in assimilation will be explored in Chapter Four, when experiences with the host country are discussed.

Asim, the forty-three year old entrepreneur, linked his Palestinian identity to his childhood experiences as a refugee in Kuwait. This was another unique characteristic of several Palestinian members of both generations—they or their families did not migrate to the United States directly after leaving Palestine, but instead fled to nearby Arab countries and lived a difficult life as refugees. The refugee experience thus becomes part of the narrative and collective memory of the group. In most cases, the children of these Palestinian refugees in the Middle East were only allowed to remain in the country past age eighteen if they secured a job, which was very difficult to do, and so most of them had no option but to leave their families and emigrate. Asim views Palestine as his homeland, and related being there and seeing what his family had lost to feeling nationless and tied to the conflict:

> I've been there before and I was introduced to everything that is ours that we can't get to now. So therefore it feels like that's where I would be if it wasn't for Kuwait as an intermediate place, where you were nobody and you had nothing. So you always question—Dad, why can't we own a house, why can't we do this and that? Why couldn't I stay after high school and go to college? He's like, son, you can't, you have to be deported because you are not a citizen and you can't stay, that's just the law in this land. I was like, where else can we go and hopefully make a future? And everybody was at that time suggesting the United States, because you had some kind of freedom and human rights. So you could come

> and become a citizen, because as a Palestinian it was very important that you please, somebody give me a passport!

Asim visited Palestine a few times, but like the others has not been back in several years because of traveling obstacles. Like Josef, Asim perceives a divide in how experiences with conflict there affect him versus his parents. They are very nostalgic for a remembered past that he lacks and, "when it's occupation and you leave, it all becomes emotional ties . . . I gave them a $300,000 home here, cars, everything. They still remember the damn little home in Palestine!" Concerning the experience of being forced out of one's home at gunpoint, he said, "If you haven't been in that, you will not feel the same way. You can't even understand. Come on, let's be realistic!" Such encounters permanently bind those who have experienced them to the conflict and the homeland.

Yasir, the forty-five year old who works in a family-owned restaurant, was born in Palestine but fled to Kuwait with his family when he was two years old. He views Palestine as his homeland because, "We had a land, we had a house, we had trees, and we have history there, so I would love to go back." Due to traveling limitations, he has only been able to return once, at age seventeen. Like Asim, he sees living there as "very important in our religion" and he dreams "of my kids learning Arabic and living in a Muslim society" with its traditional cultural norms. Also like Asim, he experienced the life of a refugee in Kuwait and says that during his seventeen years there, "we were treated worse maybe than the Israelis treat the Palestinians there." Yasir described how his parents are more overcome by the conflict because they endured it, and because the United States is more his home than theirs:

> And my parents going through that, I have a lot of sympathy. I love America; for me America's my number one so far. I lived the most here, since nineteen, so I don't know anything else. But I still have a lot of sympathy for back home. When I see my parents cry, when I see my grandparents, they remember and they show me pictures of my land—we still have land and we cannot sell it or get anything out of it.

While Ahmed, Josef, Asim, and Yasir had some direct homeland experiences on which to base their belief that their rights have been stolen from them, other members of the second generation had only the stories of their parents to connect them to homeland conflict. Like Josef, the college-age women in the sample all described how as they are growing into adulthood and learning about the conflict in a diverse college setting, they are becoming more tied to it and to their Palestinian identity. Theoretically, this timing makes sense, as adolescence and early adulthood are prime stages for the transmission of political memories (Olick & Robbins, 1998). Young adults in modern societies seek to construct integrative narratives of the self in order to create a sense of purpose and solidarity in their lives (McAdams, Diamond, de St. Aubin, & Mansfield, 1997; Schuman & Scott, 1989). With newly acquired knowledge that they can place alongside their parents' highly influential memories, these young second generation members are learning to view themselves in light of their families' existence in a conflict-ridden society.

Naimah, who is currently in college, does not view Palestine as her homeland because she has spent all her life living in the United States and in Kuwait. Also, her father, like Asim and Yasir, was ejected from Palestine as a youth and grew up nationless and powerless in Kuwait. He identifies as Palestinian, "but he considers himself American because that's the only citizenship he has." This is one clear example of how power differentials—at both the individual and the state level—shape self-identification and how transnational immigrants connect to both the home and host country (Eastmond, 2007; Georgiou, 2006; Waldinger & Fitzgerald, 2004). Unlike the extremely emotional and personalized testimonials of the other Palestinian Americans, Naimah described her connections in more detached terms. She mentioned how she has heard that her grandfather was falsely accused and jailed at some point by the Israelis, leaving her grandmother to care for all the children on her own. When asked if there are any Palestinian issues that are personally important to her, she said, "Well, I've always been kind of apathetic to politics, but when it comes to human rights issues it kind of hits me strong when I hear about how the Palestinians are treated and what happened to them." In her stories, Naimah disassociates herself from homeland and familial hardships. This is opposed to the other Palestinians' stories, where intimate details and emotional connections to the conflict were consistently expressed. Her accounts demonstrate variation in the sample and how those who have never been inside the conflict cannot fully relate to the psychological and tumultuous impact it has on the self.

"Adara" is also a college student and lives at home with her parents. She spent five years of her youth in Kuwait. Like Naimah, Adara's stories about homeland conflict were less descriptive and emotionally-laden than those told by Palestinian Americans who have directly suffered through the conflict there:

> I guess I can relate to everything that's going on there just because, like I said, family is over there and then people who have families over there . . . All my friends go back every summer, and they tell stories about people getting shot in the streets and how many funerals they go to, and there's just funeral processions that go down the streets every day.

"Hana" is a college senior who did not embrace her Palestinian heritage in the past. But like Josef and many others, she saw her identity shift as she began to learn about and identify with this side of her family more. This happened after she entered the university setting and adulthood. As she put it, "I think as I've grown up and I've become more educated and more informed, the fact that I'm a Palestinian American, and not just an American, has become more important to me." She connected her feelings about homeland conflict to her father's experiences there, noting that, "He gets very angry, and it's frustration too." She said that because he directly experienced the conflict, he reacts more and sees more overall divisions between Jews and Arabs than she does:

> For me, it hits me but it's not as much of a physical reaction. It's more I am trying to digest everything. For him, because he has so many memories and connections to that area that when he sees a picture of a tank rolling over something, or the wall being built, there's like a fire inside of him that just sparks. And I mean he gets angry sometimes. It's much more of a real response from him and much more anger, whereas I try to look at it with an open mind and just digest it before really reacting.

Raya, the university student who wears a hijab, is very outspoken about her Palestinian identity and the conflict. For her, "the biggest thing is just communication with people who are Israeli or sympathize with Israel . . . I think it's just building a bridge between two groups that are pretty much the same." Her stories were also less detailed and internalized than those given by subjects who have been to Palestine. For example, when asked if there are homeland issues that are important to her other than the conflict, she responded:

> I think the quality of life in Palestine. Just from hearing about the kind of poverty that's there, and the children that are orphaned—that's really eye-opening because I don't think I realized how many orphans there were over there.

Raya eloquently articulated an important point about how being Palestinian means that one's life will always be shaped by the conflict:

> …I think to a certain extent, for a lot of us Palestinian kids, we're born with… you know how when you're a kid you're really innocent and you can live in a sugar-spun world for a little while? But for us, we're born without that. We're born and we see the raw reality of things, and some families more than others… So I was like, okay, well this is how life really is. Not everything is beautiful. Because even when you're explaining to people "I'm Palestinian," it's different, it's a loaded statement. You can't just say "I'm Palestinian" and not follow it up with something, because it's going to come with a question. And even when you're a kid, all the other kids whose parents were immigrants, they can turn to a map and be like, this is where I'm from, this is where I'm from… And I'm like, well where I'm from is supposed to be there, and it could be this outline right here but I can't tell you because it just says the word Israel on it. So it's kind of frustrating for us when we're growing up, and it makes us tend to really separate ourselves too, which is I think is kind of part of what our problem is—is that we just kind of say, we have the burden of the world on our shoulders and that's it, and we're different than everyone else, woe to me.

As has been demonstrated, the second generation differs from their parents in that they lack ties to the "old world" and memories of conflict and are thus less likely to see the foreign country as a point of reference in evaluating their social location. Raya's statement works well to point out that although second generation Palestinian Americans are not as emotionally attached to the conflict—because their stories do not reflect personal testimonies as they do for their parents—their lives are also deeply transformed by the violence back home.

Several studies on second generation homeland attachment have discovered low transnational activism levels as compared to the active first generation (Kasinitz et al., 2002; Kibria, 2002; Rumbaut, 2002); however, as Fivush (2008) and Levitt (2009) noted, this does not meant we should dismiss the fact that the second generation has been socialized by highly engaged transnationalists. Portes et al. (2009) and Waters et al. (2010) found that the second generation largely experiences selective acculturation—they assimilate into the host country culture while preserving key elements of parental heritage and language. Additionally, some scholars (Gans, 2007; Rebhun & Lev Ari, 2010) have argued that although the second generation is not as transnationally active, they still preserve symbolic and spiritual connections to the country of origin.

When it comes to assessing how homeland conflict factors into multi-generational Palestinian identity abroad, my findings concur with those of Hammer (2005). She concluded that because the nakba was such a traumatic and fundamental historical experience for the Palestinian people, this collective memory has remained a defining aspect of Palestinian identity. For those in the diaspora, it keeps them intimately and permanently tied to the homeland. In addition, because Palestinians have had unfortunate and unique experiences with being uprooted, permanently exiled, and facing discrimination and perceived rejection, the salience of homeland conflict is all the more exacerbated in their diasporic identity.

Throughout our discussion, Raya articulated how she sees many more similarities between Palestinians and Israelis than differences, and how "separation is what makes the conflict . . . We look similar, we eat a lot of the same foods…" She did, however, acknowledge one important distinction between Palestinian Americans and Jewish Israeli Americans—the lack of power and national status that keeps Palestinians longing for a land they still cannot claim. Refugees uniquely experience a hope for return which dominates their diasporic lives (Huttunen, 2005). These exclusively Palestinian factors have a central and overriding impact on their relationship with homeland conflict and their transnational identities.

FIRST GENERATION JEWISH ISRAELI AMERICANS

While Palestinian Americans' homeland conflict stories focus mainly on the day-to-day difficulties of basic maneuverability and denial of civil liberties, Jewish Israeli Americans mostly described conflict in terms of isolated, violent incidents, such as bus bombings, or their experiences while doing mandatory military service. Both groups used memories to evince how historical circumstances have harmed their people and made their own lives difficult. They use their stories about conflict to reinforce, for both the audience and themselves, their beliefs about what is right and wrong. As Bonilla-Silva (2003) and Orbuch (1997) have suggested, personal accounts can serve a communicative and persuasive purpose as much as they reflect insights and explanations, and these multiple functions of stories can be particularly observed in my discussion of suicide bombing later in this chapter. For both Palestinian and Jewish Israeli Americans, my results confirm that the first generation feels more emotionally connected to the conflict, as it is a constitutive part of their own past. It is definitions and perceptions of conflict, levels of emotional investment, as well as the amount and degree of direct involvement, which set these two ethnic groups apart.

Liat, the graduate student who is pregnant and recently moved back to the U.S., differentiated herself from second generation Israeli Americans:

> I had a bomb go off near my home. I heard it, I heard the sirens, I called my grandma, I told her everyone's alright...you can't experience that vicariously . . . So your opinions and your ideas are going to be influenced by that.

Liat believes that those who have not lived in Israel, "whether they have Israeli parents or not, are more cognitive in their understanding of what's going on" because they lack the emotional, personal associations she gained from experiencing conflict firsthand. Liat's feelings are also stronger because her immediate family is still there. She described how seeing her husband leave for the military reserves made the conflict very real and significant for her. Liat also shared stories about Arab or Palestinian gangs who came into Jewish areas and harassed people while they were having bonfires on the beach celebrating a holiday. Liat herself was not directly involved and did not personally know anyone who was, but she feels that these violent groups, "make it unsafe for Jews and Israelis to travel within the country, and that's not fair. They beat up Jews." She sees such everyday actions and organizations as more threatening than the occasional terrorist acts because "it was organized. Because they have like scarves and they have like symbols and it was organized… there's funding going into this." When questioned about any antagonistic encounters she may have had while serving in the military, she said, "I didn't have anything directly with the conflict. I was like an HR person, so I didn't deal with that head-on."

Rachel, who is working on a PhD, was born just after the Six-Day War and lived through some intensified periods of Arab-Israeli conflict during her early childhood. She learned to develop strong defenses against reacting to violence "when I was a child, having to just not think about it all the time." When prompted about experiences with conflict, the stories she recalled were mostly distant ones; for example, she spoke about "what happened in Ramallah, with the lynch thing. That had a huge effect on me." This incident took place about ten years earlier and involved Jewish soldiers getting lost and winding up in Ramallah where they were attacked and killed. There is a famous image from this event of a Palestinian showing the murdered men's blood upon his hands. Rachel mentioned how when she was young, "there were a lot of bus bombings, sometimes on buses we were always on, and some people that I knew were around or sometimes hurt." Events like these make her afraid to be in Israel. When asked about her military service, she told me, "I was actually in intelligence and it wasn't the main thing we were worried about, you know, countries, it was not influential."

Maytal, a post-doctoral student and mother of four children, never realized that she was living a stressful life until she emigrated from Israel. Like Rachel, she learned to cope with the underlying tension created by the ever-present threat of conflict by suppressing it. Experiencing life in America has made it difficult for her to imagine returning to Israel. Her firsthand narratives were centered on her life there just before she left, during the heightened conflict of the Second Intifada:

> When I sat in Jerusalem and did my PhD there, I could hear the sirens of each ambulance. Also, 2002 was the worst year, I think. So everyday you'd know where the bomb is. We really lived the stressed life, although living there it didn't seem like it, only when we came here. Before we came here I wanted to buy shoes for my daughter in the mall in Jerusalem. I remember rushing in, getting the shoes, running out. And I thought that's normal, I never had a problem with it. Only coming here and my daughter started going to the mall and we'd go for hours and never be scared, I thought, oh my God, we lived a very, very stressful life there, on a daily basis.

She also spoke about a nail bomb set off in 2002 at a Hebrew University cafeteria, a building where her father worked; this too made her fearful about life in Israel.[2]

Moshe described the direct violence he faced while serving in the Israeli military:

> I was in Lebanon when in the army. I saw bombings and people die over there and one day I woke up and the room was still shaking, and you could still smell the smell of the weapons, and I was this close to being gone. And my friend who was with me got very crazy.

All four of these respondents also mentioned how those who have not existed in a combative society cannot relate to it in the same way that they do. Maytal believes that others can choose to feel less involved in the conflict, whereas she does not have that choice because, "You know, the conflict *is* me."

Noam, the immunologist, explained how living through the major wars of Israel's past "plus the fact that I was in the military and all of that, I think that those things had an influence. Definitely they did in terms of the conflict." He described, just as Ahmed did, how close together everything is in this small land. Being there and seeing the

---

[2] This example hit home for me: I myself ate in this cafeteria many times while studying abroad in Jerusalem in 1998. I also knew a woman who was killed in that very explosion; she was there with me in 1998 and then returned to the same school years later for a different academic program.

actual distances "made it very visual" and verified for him just why Israel needs to maintain its borders, for safety's sake.

Tzipora, who spent her youth in Central and South America as well as Israel, was very emotive when telling her stories about homeland conflict. She listed the cousins who were killed in a suicide bomb and those killed during the Yom Kippur War, which she also lived through as a young girl. The conflict had profound repercussions for her, as her father worked for the Israeli government:

> I was going to sleep dressed because I needed to run to the bomb shelters in the middle of the night. And my dad worked for the Israeli embassy... I couldn't open a toy or a gift without taking it through x-rays because it could be a bomb. And I'm talking years ago, right? Forty years ago. Or I grew up knowing that I can't pick up a pen from the floor because it could be a bomb. Up to this day, I don't let my kids pick up everything from the floor because even though I don't think I was traumatized then—it wasn't scary, it was normal—but it has affected how I see it.

She is concerned about second generation Israeli Americans today because "there is a young generation that we created, making them live very comfortable and not aware that they need to care—the need to be global citizens! And they have no need, they don't see that." In contrast, she described how being there, in the conflicted homeland, bonded her for life not just to the Israeli-Palestinian situation but to ethnic strife across the world.

Tzipora also discussed a media-sensationalized and highly contentious issue—suicide bombing. Many of the Jewish Israeli Americans mentioned suicide bombing as a typical instance of conflict there, and all unequivocally expressed their condemnation of this form of assault. Several of the Palestinian American subjects also expressed their disapprobation of this kind of resistance and labeled it as counteractive and pointless in the long run. They did, however, differ from the Jewish Israelis in that they were able to see some of the underlying motivations and reasoning behind these desperate acts, whereas Jewish Israelis, like Tzipora, cannot and will not attempt to excuse or empathize with suicide bombers:

> ...When there is a suicide bomber, maybe I will judge as unacceptable, right? I think that there are many ways, financial ways... there are many ways of punishing a country but not killing people. And it will be different for them. They will say there is a reason for this person to kill themselves, to be a suicide bomber. I won't agree and that's why we differ, because I think we all have choices of doing bad things or good things, and we will decide. I think that there are many, even if you walk around the corner, who are underprivileged, but they won't decide to harm those who are not giving them a job and kill themselves. It's a choice. So whenever someone will justify violence, I will stop identifying with them.

Some Palestinian Americans in my sample expressed frustration with the negative reputation suicide bombers give the overwhelming majority of non-violent Palestinians. However, despite their denunciation of these acts of violence, they additionally acknowledged some reasons behind the acts—namely a sense of futility and extreme despair at having lost everything. Hassan articulated this perspective:

> Technically, sociologists, technically they say when you put people in a situation like this, due to human nature it creates a complete outrageous behavior. I don't know, it's what we see when many of the Palestinian, when they go start becoming suicide bombers. It's the result of this inhumane treatment, so the people feel like they have nothing to lose. They are dead while they're living, you know, may as well be dead and kill as many people with them. It's desperation, exactly.

These divergent understandings of suicide bombings by ethnic group exemplify the importance of discussing identity in "collective" terms, as we are always influenced by the groups to which we belong, and thus our contrasting perspectives never exist entirely outside of the group's pull. Again, it is the primary agents of socialization, such as the family, through which we accrue these disparate mindsets. The mainstream stereotype linking Palestinians to terrorism and suicide bombing was vocalized by Moshe, who said, "Teaching kids to hate Jews, hate Israelis... they teach them at young ages how to go out and be a bomber. This is crazy! I mean, why? What good does it do?" Liat made similar generalized statements:

> And today I feel like the Palestinian side is not making as much of an effort as it should, especially seeing that the generations that have grown up are still so anti-Semitic and are still educated by… so the subtraction—you have five Jews, you kill two, how many are left? That's a subtraction lesson! And they have it in their education books.

These mass categorizations impact how Palestinians identify with their ethnicity, as it is known that ethnic and racial identities can be partially imposed upon the individual (Gans, 2007; Zimmermann et al., 2007). In most cases, I found that Palestinian Americans are conscious of and concerned about being labeled terrorists and suicide bombers, especially when disclosing their ethnicity to strangers.

In accordance with theoretical expectations, several first generation Jewish Israeli Americans recognized that their relationship with the conflict has fluctuated over time, based on their stage in life, and also on the current state of affairs back home. Gil was one of several who mentioned how during the rule of Yitzhak Rabin there was a different collective mindset: "In the mid-'90s the peace process was going on and I think that had a major influence. I think young people especially . . . were very hopeful towards the future." Unfortunately, after the assassination of the Prime Minister, the peace process fell apart and the conflict worsened. Gil was fearful during this change:

> Once terrorism started, it felt more like a real danger because I wasn't exposed to war really before that, actively. But then once terrorism started, then you couldn't really be detached from it anymore, just live your own life. I know it influenced how I feel… I still believe in peace, I maybe just didn't think it was as simple as before.

I discovered an interesting ethnic group distinction involving experiences with the Other in the homeland. Gil, Efrat, and several other Jewish Israelis, who lived in predominantly Jewish communities in Israel, mentioned to me that they had very little direct interaction and contact with Palestinians other than the occasional service-sector transaction or dealing with them in military service. In contrast, the

Palestinians I spoke with had constant and mostly negative encounters with Israelis. The Israelis they knew were border patrolmen who interrogated them, or IDF soldiers who entered their villages and assumed total authority and control. According to conflict theory, peaceful, everyday encounters with the Other facilitate coexistence and resolution of conflict, whereas limited and negative interactions exacerbate it (Memmi, 1965; Simmel, 1955). Jewish-Israelis' very limited exchanges and Palestinians' frequent and consistently adverse ones thus work to partially explain how the conflict is perpetuated at the individual level.

There were a few exceptions to this pattern, including Rachel, who asserted that homeland conflict occurs predominantly at the group level, and not at the personal level:

> I mean, I worked with them in the Israeli television in Arabic, so there were a lot of Palestinians working there, and there were very good relations, I think. On the day-to-day basis everything felt friendly and natural... So yeah, I think [the problem is] not [at] the one-on-one [level].

Ofer grew up less than half a mile from the Lebanese border. His encounters with Arabs throughout his youth greatly influenced his understanding of the conflict, again supporting conflict theory claims about the positive functions of increased interaction:

> I've been in Lebanon during the war before, so I saw Lebanon and I saw Lebanese. I have Palestinian friends that I worked with before, Arab Israelis. I left during the First Intifada and I have many Palestinian friends. I used to speak some Arabic but I lost it. But these people that live maybe ten miles from where I grew up, they didn't want to have anything to do with this conflict. They just want to have their own lives. They want to earn a decent living. They have houses, they have families, and they want it to be quiet.

Ofer continues to be influenced by these initial exchanges; this is demonstrated by his ongoing participation in a local, inter-ethnic Middle Eastern peace organization.

SECOND GENERATION JEWISH ISRAELI AMERICANS

Leah, the medical student, believes that there are several types of group-level conflicts occurring simultaneously in Israel—from the Arab-Israeli to the Sephardim-Ashkenazi, and most important to her, the orthodox-secular divide. She believes that "a lot of other conflicts in Israeli society are overlooked because of that one [Arab-Israeli], because when you're at war, you can't really focus on the economic and social issues in your country." She remembers traveling to Israel several times in her youth with her parents, and her insights demonstrate the immense influence parents have on children's understandings of conflict:

> Probably my reactions to things are reflecting how my parents react to them, just because I grew up with them. So I think their perspective, since we go to Israel so much and there's always conflict, was you just, [you] can't let it affect your plans. I mean obviously you're not going to travel in a war-torn area, but there were lots of times that we went that there was active conflict going on.

When asked if there were any experiences she had in Israel that stand out as significant for how she relates to the conflict, she said that there were none.

Like Leah, Dalia, who is currently an undergraduate in college, also traveled to Israel frequently with her parents throughout her youth; she too did not share any personal stories of homeland conflict experiences when prompted. She contrasted herself with her mother, describing her mother as "a lot more suspicious and wary" due to her past in Israel which included living through the Six-Day War. Dalia illustrated this point with an example:

> One time there was like a backpack sitting somewhere and somebody had left for like just a few minutes… and she was like, "Who left that there and why is it there?" And I was like, "Mom, it's just a book bag," and she was like, "Yeah, but you never know what could be in it."

She also sees her mother as much more inflexible and intense in her feelings about how the conflict should be resolved—"she's like just get out, leave us alone."

Zev also agrees that living in the homeland makes all the difference in how one views the conflict and her or his own identity:

> And it's the sort of thing that you just sort of grow to—once you live in Israel, you feel like this is your country and that's it. Because before I went to Israel, I wasn't necessarily Israeli. I mean, I was Israeli by the fact that my mom was Israeli, but it's different.

He explained why he does not see the dispute with the Palestinians as a conflict, although he does see the recent war with Lebanon as one:

> I think that the fact that the Palestinian-Israeli conflict has been happening for such a long time, it's no longer a conflict for me anymore. I think the Lebanese with the Hezbollah was more of a conflict . . . and Palestine it's not really a war, it's just war on terror, which is completely different. Especially because it's just a different style of fighting—it's more preventative then it is trying to attack someone, which is what we did before the Hezbollah because we were forced to. But against the Palestinian terrorists, the suicide bombers, I mean, we're pretty much trying to prevent them from coming into the central territory rather than trying to attack them when they do something, although we do that as well in order to prevent… I mean, it's really just messed up…

Zev's father served in the military for his entire career, including during the 1967 Arab-Israeli War. His father assesses the conflict from a military perspective, focusing on what he thinks are the best actions for the army to take. This predisposition to see Israel through a military lens has clearly been absorbed by Zev, as most of what he discussed in relation to the conflict was linked to IDF decisions. Zev voluntarily served in the army in 2006, not long before our interview: "Well, I mean, when I support the conflict, like in the war in Lebanon, I feel like I have to do something to support it really. I can't just sit around and just look at it happening, and that's why I went to Israel this past summer." All of his Israeli friends were enlisted at the time, as every Israeli citizen must serve in the army for at least two years after high school, and he felt he needed to share this experience with them. Zev did not recall any immediate experiences with conflict, even during his military service.

Zev, like Tzipora and many other Jewish Israelis I interviewed, cannot relate at all to the actions of suicide bombers and thinks it is because of them that the conflict with the Palestinians is never-ending:

> How can we end it? The wall [between Israel proper and the West Bank] is the only way to prevent more suicide bombings. They are just going to have a wall and you're going to have suicide bombers on the other side just packing up. Just a lot more suicide bombers who want to get in, but there's the wall that's blocking it. But that's not going to change anything, the hatred is still there. You take away the wall and there's still going to be suicide bombers going in with bigger numbers. It's actually maybe a better thing that we're shooting them now because then there aren't that many. If we take away the wall then they're just all going to go right in.

As opposed to many Palestinian Americans, who disapprove of this tactic but nevertheless see the humanity and suffering behind it, Zev clearly views suicide bombers in a more abstract, detached way and his focus is on how to stop them, whether with walls or guns. (Here there is potential evidence of my Jewish background impacting the research process: if Zev assumed that I was Jewish, he may have felt more comfortable making comments about killing Palestinians. Likewise, this may in part explain why I did not hear similar types of comments about Israelis or Jews from any Palestinian respondents.).

David, the thirty-four year old dentist, also expressed his opinion that the erection of a wall along the West Bank was a necessary tactic for keeping suicide bombers from infiltrating Israel.[3] David admits that the conflict foments his animosity towards the Palestinians and that he perceives significant group-level divides:

---

[3]While Zev and David view the wall purely in terms of protection, critics of this barrier, which is nearing completion as of this writing, argue that it violates international law and is motivated by Israeli expansionism and resource control and Palestinian annexation (Chomsky, 2010; Ellis, 2009).

> I think Israelis are more of a negotiating group, and the Palestinians are more under the impression that they have to use forceful or tactical suicide, murder kind of things to get their point across. I mean, I'd rather see people sitting at a table for a year or two, working things out on paper, giving maybe land here and land there, instead of… they just feel they have to do everything with violence. It's just the wrong way they're going about it, totally.

David asserted that the majority of Palestinians "are for that type of insurgence" and those who do not endorse it are not speaking out against it as they should. Like other second generation Jewish Israeli Americans I interviewed, David went to Israel with his family many times in his youth but did not recount any stories of experiencing conflict directly.

As previously mentioned, Sasha, who works in the high tech industry, did not recall enduring or even thinking about immediate conflict while she lived in Israel as a teenager. Her perspectives reflect those of first generation Israelis, as she was able to downplay the threat of violence in Israel and maintain what felt like a normal life there. Also akin to first generation Jewish Israelis, now that she has lived in America and can reflect back on her Israeli existence, Sasha finds it "kind of frightening how living there you get very used to it, like bus bombs going off and stuff like that." Her stories of conflict were mostly impersonal, and even her disparagement of Palestinians seemed distanced: "…because you hear about a lot more terrorism rather than military warfare, I guess. You know, attacking civilians doesn't seem cool to me." Echoing Dalia's discussion of her mother, Sasha said that

> because [my mother is] a first generation Israeli, she definitely has a lot stronger feelings about things than I do . . . She's very pro-Israel and . . . most definitely biased against Palestinians and Arabs in general.

Shai is distinct among the other second generation Jewish Israelis because he spends every summer visiting his parents in Israel proper and also promotes conflict resolution from within the West Bank. He sees himself as "having moved from a non-Zionist to an 'anti-Zionist.' I see myself, my identity, as opposed to the fundamental basis of the

Israeli state." His connection to the conflict was largely shaped by his father: "My dad was an activist and I remember going to demonstrations when I was seven years old, shouting 'Two states for two peoples!'"

Shai's descriptions of experiencing conflict in Israel and the occupied territories were direct and poignant. He referred to an instance when he was participating in a demonstration in the West Bank and instead of using the regular stun guns and tear gas, the Israeli army

> opened fire with rubber-coated lead bullets within ten seconds of us arriving at the army line. An acquaintance of mine was shot with a rubber bullet in the head from a distance of 10 meters away and had to have part of his brain removed.

He discussed several other engaging memories of conflict, mostly from his experiences over the past couple of years:

> I was in Haifa for part of the time and I was in the West Bank for a lot of the time as well. So I was going from having missiles raining down on my hometown, to West Bank demonstrations which were very, very pro-Hezbollah, and to anti-war demonstrations in Tel Aviv which tried to balance the two. And so I also had cousins up in the north very much near the border; two of my cousins were in the army station near the border. So yeah, I was very much involved in that conflict.

Shai described his view of the situation in one of the occupied territories:

> The West Bank actually was extremely pro-Hezbollah. You had Hezbollah fighting songs in every shop corner, there were Hezbollah flags everywhere, pictures of [Hezbollah leader] Hassan Nasrallah everywhere. And I participated in demonstrations which were, um… strongly against the Israeli reaction, and in many cases pretty pro-Hezbollah. I was extremely uncomfortable in these demonstrations. It was difficult being in Ramallah with Palestinians waving Hezbollah flags, coming from Haifa.

> By the time we got to Israel and I had met my cousins and they invited me to go up north, and the next day was the first serious missile attack on Haifa and there were eight people killed in a railway station which is not particularly far from my house.

Another of Shai's unique qualities is that he has experienced immediate conflict within the context of both ethnic groups—he has been a victim on both sides. He has many friends and cousins currently serving in the Israeli military as well as many friends living within the occupied territories. He has close contact and relationships within both sides of the conflict, and thus can arguably see more clearly the complexities and gray areas involved.

When Shai first began his volunteerism in the occupied territories, he realized how unaware he was of what real life on the inside was like:

> I came for the first ten days into a village which just had… all their water sources were cut off; they were cut off from agricultural land. I was one of the first Israelis to be there since the beginning of Intifada, and that was extremely difficult. I ended up becoming good friends with a guy whose brother was a suicide bomber. And I had no idea about his history when he invited me to his house, had dinner, there was a picture of his brother and we got into a conversation and it turned out that his brother was killed on his way to blow himself up in Haifa . . . The army caught him and he was killed on the way. And my first reaction was stunned silence but then I [realized] this person is someone I've just become friends with over the last week, and what his brother did or didn't do is not linked to whether he has the right to live an adequate life, whether he has a right to be able to feed his children. And so my awareness very much changed. That was one of the defining moments but there have been many others since.

For Shai this was a transformative moment where the issue of suicide bombing became less abstract and incorporated into his overall understanding of the conflict. In Shai's particular example we observe support for two important theoretical themes. The first is that collective meanings and memories are drastically selective and subjective (Fivush, 2008; Keightley, 2010; Langfield, 2009; Misztal, 2010; Olick, 1999; Ram, 2009; Yerushalmi, 1982). Second, we can see how interfacing with the Other involved in a conflict reduces the sense of separation and opposition (Smooha, 1998; Worchel, 2005). Like Raya and Gameel, Shai believes that bridging the gap between Palestinians and Israelis is the only way to end the conflict. He thus condemns the building of walls between Israel and Palestine. One of Shai's most powerful stories recalled centered on his volunteerism in Nablus. During an Israeli military incursion, the Palestinian children were yelling at Shai and his companion and chasing them. They stopped and explained to the children why they were there; the next day, Shai said, ten times more children flocked to them and "we were the most popular kids in town." This instance showed Shai how easily perceptions can be altered and stereotypes overcome through contact, especially with the youngest generation.

CONCLUSIONS

Respondents' narratives and shared memories show that for Palestinian Americans, past involvement with homeland conflict often causes ongoing pain and identity effects—trickling down even to the second generation—born from permeating experiences with restriction, poverty, harassment, and fear for one's life. In comparison, Jewish Israeli Americans reported a somewhat paradoxical mixture of "normal life must go on" sentiment combined with recognition (sometimes only post-migration) that they were affected by the underlying, ever-present tension caused by the looming conflict and the knowledge that violence could erupt anywhere, anytime. While many members of this group offered few specific recollections of personal encounters with conflict, several cited bombings or other attacks that stuck in their minds.

For both groups, the first generation's telling and retelling of personal stories of conflict has a discernible impact on their children. However, this mechanism was arguably more visible in second generation Palestinians' emotional depictions of shared family memories. Second generation Jewish Israelis told fewer personalized stories about homeland conflict. And missing from the accounts of both generations of Jewish Israeli Americans was the Palestinians' particularized sense of ongoing suffering resulting from memories of forced expulsion and knowledge of what life is like for those still living under occupation.

Two additional elements play an important role in how Palestinian and Jewish Israeli American identities are constructed and negotiated via perceptions of homeland conflict. First is their use of, and attitudes toward, media and other sources of knowledge about current conflict; this is the central theme of the next chapter. Second is how each group perceives the host country, the United States, and its role in the Israeli-Palestinian conflict—the crux of Chapter Four.

CHAPTER 3:

Sources of Homeland Conflict Information

In Chapter Two I examined how personal narratives and accounts about homeland conflict continue to shape the identities of immigrants and their children, and—relying upon key insights from the fields of social memory theory and narratives/storytelling methods— concluded that these recalled experiences do have a continuous and significant impact on identity. Their primary effect, of course, is on the first generation, but they also influence the second generation through the intergenerational sharing of memories and stories. In this chapter, I continue to ask how distant conflict shapes identity by exploring the influence of sources of information about current homeland conflict.

Migrant families tend to lead transnational lives. They maintain social ties across borders, travel back and forth, and participate in homeland and host country politics (Langfield, 2009; Levitt & Waters, 2002; Portes & Rumbaut, 2006; Rebhun & Lev Ari, 2010; Waters & Ueda, 2007). My respondents' main sources of up-to-date information proved to be, as I had anticipated, transnational social networks and media coverage. Family and friends still living in the homeland serve continual and important roles as agents of socialization for these respondents; in relation to the conflict, they function as valuable informants due to their immediacy and access to local, more detailed information. I discovered through the interviews that homeland conflict is a prevalent topic of discussion for subjects and their social networks in Israel/Palestine. Homeland conflict thus works in both directions—it keeps people in the diaspora talking to their homeland contacts and by doing so reinforces the role of the conflict in their diasporic identities. Mass media and ethnic organizations are secondary socializing agents; these institutions work to inform the diaspora about homeland conflict on a more regular and consistent basis (El-Aswad, 2006; Georgiou, 2006; Gillespie, 2006; Matar, 2006; Viswanath & Ka-man Lee, 2007). Media also have an impact on collective memories. As we will see, the ways they selectively frame the conflict shape how diasporic individuals' remember and relate to it (Georgiou, 2006).

As for generational differences in information usage, I originally expected that first generation members of both populations would have more dense and extensive social networks in Israel/Palestine, as they had established ties to family and friends while living there. Of course, the strength and longevity of these connections would depend on individual characteristics, such as length of time lived in the homeland and efforts to maintain relationships post-migration. I surmised that the second generation would have less access to personal sources of information in the homeland, as they had spent limited to no time there and most likely retain most relations with friends and family there through their parents. In lieu of direct contacts, the second generation, I assumed, would rely more so on their parents and mainstream, mostly American media sources for information. I also anticipated that they would, as a whole, be informed about conflict less often and less intensively than their parents. However, since the media have played an important role over time in creating an international image of Israel and Palestine as a place full of violence, where one's life is in constant jeopardy (Dunsky, 2008; Said, 1979), and since it is known that media representations have an impact on the attitudes of those with little or no contrasting experiences (Gilens, 1999; Kamalipour, 1997), I expected that the conflict would be the overriding central group issue and concern of the second generation, who have been influenced by this media coverage. As for the first generation, with their direct homeland experiences, I originally hypothesized that they would regard a multitude of events back home as important (such as political divisions, economic concerns, and environmental issues) besides the significant Israeli-Palestinian conflict, and to a greater extent than their children. I did find consistent support for my expectations, as I will demonstrate; however, the processes involved proved to be much more complex and varied than I had originally anticipated.

First, in accordance with Chapter Two, although I did discover through my interviews that media portrayals have a greater impact on the second generation than the first, it was, for the second generation, nevertheless parents' memories and narratives that primarily shaped their relationship with homeland conflict. How the first generation discussed and explained the Israeli-Palestinian conflict throughout their upbringing laid the foundation for the second generation's understandings and connections to the conflict as adults.

Second, differences in information source usage and resulting perceptions of conflict turned out to vary not as much by generation, but rather by ethnic group. Reflecting basic findings from the previous chapter, Jewish Israeli Americans of both generations regularly discussed how the Israeli-Palestinian conflict was just one important aspect in the homeland. But for Palestinian Americans, conflict was a more or less all-consuming concern. Palestinians' homeland lives were always permeated by conflict, as it encroached upon their day-to-day reality and livelihood. An additional ethnic group-level factor is the widely perceived media bias against the Arab world—including Palestinians—which is often represented as prone to fundamentalism and violence (Gold & Bozorgmehr, 2007; Marvasti & McKinney, 2004; Noakes & Wilkins, 2002; Reich, 1991; Said, 1979). These group-level distinctions demonstrate the multiplicity involved in transnationalism and identity due to contextual factors such as migrant population characteristics and the impact of the state and politics.

FIRST GENERATION PALESTINIAN AMERICANS

Hearing about current episodes of homeland conflict has an immense impact on Palestinian subjects. Emotionally-evocative issues are known to have the greatest influence on identity, and ethnic identity is most commonly expressed in terms of feelings (such as nostalgia, sadness, and solidarity) (Gans, 2007). This was clearly the case for the first generation Palestinian Americans. For example, when asked how hearing about an episode of conflict affects him, Mansur replied:

> It varies. Sometimes I live with pain and I know it affects my health, and so I internalize it. So that occasionally happens. Sometimes I'm not even willing to read anything about it. I don't want to hear the news. I don't want to read the news… So sometimes I try to sort of shrink and put myself in this little circle. I don't want to know… there's nothing I can do about

> it… and then sometimes… and it is like a struggle; it's an internal struggle. And then in a few days I sort of wake up and say, I wanted to know. And then I start learning, and it sort of cycles.

This time in relation to receiving information about the conflict, Mansur referred again to his previously-cited notion of Palestine as a weight to be carried:

> And I know it's a burden. It creates actually a conflict between you and the country you love . . . So either you jump in it and you become close to the Palestinians… or you build a boundary so you don't want to know, you don't want to be involved.

Safia also discussed this pattern of initially needing to know and then being unable to handle knowing about the hardships experienced by Palestinians:

> I have Al Jazeera on and off. I get it, then I get so depressed that I can't even function. So we cancel it, then we get it again, and then for a few months I get so depressed, and then I cancel it. It's on and off.

Another trend observed in the first generation was that over time, as things have worsened in Palestine, many have lost hope and have accordingly become less involved in and knowledgeable about the conflict. This pattern supports the notion that both identity and transnational activism are dynamic across the lifecourse, depending on personal and public circumstances. Mansur recollected:

> I do believe that this feeling started about seven, eight years ago… I think with the second Bush administration I really started to believe that there is no political solution to this problem. And I just reached a point where I just lost hope in a way.

Umar discussed a different trajectory for the development of identification with and understanding of the conflict (a pattern previously cited in Chapter Two in the second generation): "As we grow older, we get more educated and we get more in contact, and we get more realization of the facts and the truths, or close enough anyways."

An important reason that hearing about conflict can be so unbearable for Palestinian Americans is the presence of family and friends in Palestine—people they know are suffering but cannot help. Some respondents, such as Hassan, even retain land there that they consider a second home and try to visit often. (Unfortunately, the Gaza closure happening at the time of our interview kept Hassan from his annual visit.) Mansur has brothers, sisters, nieces, and nephews in Palestine, as well as uncles and aunts. He comes from a small village where everyone knows each other, and he feels a strong bond with the town and stays informed about it as best as he can.

> I feel personally responsible for doing my best to help the Palestinians because it's my family, it's my people. Yes, I am an American citizen, but the American way is to help those who need… My brother is there and suddenly he's the school principal and he could not collect his salary, so he's hungry, his family is hungry. So this is a moral responsibility.

Mansur draws a distinction between himself and others, such as the second generation, who can choose not to know what is happening in Palestine. Meanwhile, he cannot escape needing to know about the conflict because of his roots and ties to the land. He believes that those less directly connected to the conflict can live in more peace and with greater ease than he can imagine.

The conflict is ever-present in Safia's daily life: "I mean, the truth is that it's always there. It never leaves. My ears are tuned to what's being said about the conflict. It never goes away." Safia accesses family in Palestine for information on the state of the conflict on a daily basis. She frequently hears their stories of personal encounters with conflict:

> My sister is married to a Palestinian whose family is there and he goes frequently, and they are on the phone all the time because his family's there. So then she'll say, they took the land that's on this mountain today, or his sister cannot live in Jerusalem. I mean she just tells me some stories that sound

> bizarre. She does not have Jerusalem ID, so she cannot ride in a car with [her husband]. She has to walk her daughter to school but if she ever gets caught in a car she gets fined a thousand dollars. So I hear those firsthand stories from relatives that are in contact.

Gameel, like Safia and Mansur, believes that having roots in Palestine permanently binds a person to the conflict and to staying informed about it:

> I think that being a Palestinian or a Palestinian American…you can't help but have this… I mean this is part of who you become—is what's going on over there. So you are listening to the news, you are trying to work towards doing something that will get people to hear what's going on.

Members of the first generation rely on personal homeland sources of information more often than their children; however, they also access international media sources constantly and more frequently than the second generation. The news is always on in Palestinian immigrants' homes and plays a central role in their everyday lives as transnational families (Gillespie, 2006; Matar, 2006). When the conflict gets heated, their media consumption levels soar (Gillespie, 2006). The most prominent resource mentioned by almost every first generation Palestinian American was Al Jazeera. It is common for Palestinian Americans to get satellite television so that they can watch this main Arab news station. Sakr has suggested that the proliferation of Arab satellite channels has contributed to a sense of pan-Arab identity, as individuals across the globe watch the same programs simultaneously (1999). Media consumption is thereby not just an individual but a transnational cultural activity (Georgiou, 2006). Al Jazeera is the preferred Middle East station for my respondents because the coverage concentrates on issues they perceive as more relevant and uses their native language; but even more importantly, first generation Palestinian Americans prefer Al Jazeera because they share the common view that American media are biased against their people and thus cover the conflict inaccurately. Although some scholarship has suggested that this opinion may not be unfounded (Bishara, 2008; Dunsky, 2008; Ellis, 2009; Gillespie, 2006; Matar, 2006; Noakes & Wilkins, 2002), respondents also seem likely to be exhibiting a trend known in the literature as "hostile media" perception (e.g. Ariyanto, Hornsey, & Gallois, 2007; Eveland & Shah, 2003), in which conflict coverage is seen as favoring the other side. I later demonstrate Jewish Israeli subjects displaying the same outlook on media.

Palestinian Americans also commonly asserted that American press lacks depth. "It just seems more like it's for entertainment than it is for getting news across," as Gameel put it. Mansur added, "I don't really believe the media is fair [here]. I don't think the media is telling the truth. That's why I try to get my sources from another source—Al Jazeera." Safia had similar views and noted:

> I feel like it's my mission to educate people, because I believe it's a very distorted picture that they get of who we are. They think of us as very, very violent, vicious people that just want to kill all Jews…

As she feels obligated to help overcome negative stereotyping of Palestinians through teaching others, Safia exemplifies here how media can augment the salience of diasporic identification (Georgiou, 2006). Over time, as the media have selectively framed the conflict and shaped Americans' perceptions of it, they have also helped revitalize the ethnic identities of some Palestinian Americans who feel compelled to inform the public that they are not supporters of violence (Georgiou, 2006).

Hassan believes that all people hear in the news, from which they derive stereotypes, is

> Palestinian bombing, the suicide, mostly the killings of the Israeli children, you know… "They just want to kill all Jews." And "The Jews are protecting themselves" . . . [The U.S. media], it's unbalanced. You know, it's not like they're fair when it comes to the Palestinian issue.

Umar sees the mass media as biased, inaccurate, and not to be trusted. "I think the media is a bunch of baloney, personally. Again, it's who controls that media and what picture do they want you to know or see."

Gameel discussed distorted media representations of Palestinians in greater detail:

> The Palestinian story is not something that gets aired very often, and when it does it appears to be very skewed. The media, in my opinion, tends to be... when people make fanatical statements they report that a lot, but when people come and speak in measured tones you never hear it.

He went on to give an example—underreported peace talks involving the King of Jordan versus the well-publicized Iranian president's rant against Jews—and stressed that in the face of media discrimination against Arabs, it is important for Palestinians to educate Americans: "A lot of other people sadly follow whatever the media tells them, so it becomes this everybody-in-that-group-is-this-way."

Hassan was once asked to be a guest on a local television news program and speak about the Palestinian-Israeli conflict. He felt discriminated against as the reporter tilted the conversation toward mass generalizations of Palestinians as supporters of suicide bombing:

> And he was so quick. I didn't like their questions. I mean, they asked me... I was there to talk about the conflict, but all of the sudden he's asking me, "Do you approve of suicide bombings?" I mean, what am I, a suicide bomber? But I was on live television, so I tried to conduct myself, trying to answer questions that he's not asking. But then, after the show I really protested. I told him, "You're stereotyping, and for a journalist like yourself..."

Later, the same journalist apologized and gave him a more open platform to debate the issue with a prominent Jew from the community. However, Hassan noted that while the Jewish man was being interviewed in a high-end hotel conference room, he was placed at an anchor desk at the local news station, which he feels speaks to their respective status in American society.

Interestingly, several of the Palestinian Americans interviewed mentioned that they seek out American and even Israeli media sources, not for factual information but to see how other potentially biased sides frame the conflict. Umar told me about how he listens to AM radio station programs such as Rush Limbaugh's:

> They're always one-sided. I listen to them not because I disagree or agree; I listen just to hear what people say. I've

> called one time, I've called twice and three and four times. And they screened my phone call and when they hear what I want to say they'll put me on hold. One time they put me on hold for forty-five minutes and another time they put me on hold for an hour and a half. I forgot that I was on hold—I left the house! And so is it biased? You're doggone right it's biased!

Gameel remains deeply informed about the conflict and while he does hear stories from contacts back in Palestine, he additionally relies on a wide variety of media to keep him up to date. When asked which sources he relies on to find out about homeland conflict, Gameel cited several—*Ha-Aretz*, *The Jerusalem Post*, *The Jordan Times*, BBC, NPR, Al-Jazeera's website, CNN, and *The Financial Times*. The only major news medium he avoids is Fox, which he says "just makes me too upset." This Fox media caveat was quite common among Palestinians subjects.

A few first generation Palestinians were active in pan-ethnic organizations supporting the Palestinian cause. For them, these groups are a useful addition to homeland social networks and media as an information source about homeland conflict. Active participation in these organizations also varies across the lifecourse, depending on factors such as the intensity of the conflict, personal free time, and, as I will discuss in the next chapter, receptivity conditions for Palestinians in the host country. Safia and Hassan are involved in organizations aimed at resolving the conflict through inter-ethnic contact and collaboration, such as dialogue groups. Safia even started her own group, which includes herself and two other mothers who practice Judaism and Christianity respectively; together they publicly speak about the conflict and work towards peace. Gameel mentioned his membership in a few popular Arab organizations, including the Arab American Institute—which keeps him informed about Palestine-related discussions and actions by the American government—and the more active Arab American Anti-Discrimination committee.

As for generational differences in media usage, Safia believes that the second generation "probably rely more on local sources here, like the news. And most likely they may not speak Arabic, so Al Jazeera won't be that useful to them." She also thinks that hearing about homeland conflict matters to them but "it's a lot more painful when you are first generation and you've lived there." Mansur's response is aligned with Safia's. He claims that while his main news source is an Arab one, his children access mainstream and often internet-based American sources, such as Google News, even though they speak Arabic and could potentially use the same resources as him.[1] Although his children focus on Palestinian news less than him, Mansur has noticed that they "pay more attention… reading things related to Palestine more than if there is something on [for example] Thailand." Umar also believes that his children are less invested in the conflict, and even suspects they may find reports of violence against Palestinians no more notable than media accounts of other conflicts:

> So they don't know any difference. And now as they get older, like my son is graduating from high school tomorrow, what's he got on his mind? Nothing. He has lost nothing; he never lost his home. He hears of my stories… but he feels the pain that the Palestinians feel when he watches TV, I reckon, just like you would feel if you watched anybody getting killed or shot.

SECOND GENERATION PALESTINIAN AMERICANS

As first generation respondents surmise, the second generation experience life in America differently than their parents, as they struggle to blend in while incorporating ethnic perspectives taught to them by both their parents and the media. While group-level conflict narratives and parental memories have the greatest impact on second generation ethnic identities, media coverage of the conflict also has a perceptible effect. As Gillespie (2006) noted, media is a socialization agent—it generates a place where identity and feelings of belonging are

---

[1] Electronic forms of media, especially the internet, are increasingly favored, especially by those in the diaspora and younger cohorts (Georgiou, 2006; Matar, 2006). The internet, it is argued, has created new transnational space that transcends physical divides and unites dispersed ethnic group members (Siapera, 2010). New technologies thus play an important role in shaping and preserving transnational ties and identities, and this trend is only expected to increase over time and across generations (Georgiou, 2006; Gillespie, 2006; Gowricharn, 2009).

recurrently questioned, processed, and fortified. This is especially the case for younger cohorts.

Raya thinks that the conflict is "very ingrained into my identity, and that's why I am so politically active to a certain extent." She felt as if she "was growing up in the Middle East, just because I went to private school for eight years, and it was a private Islamic school that's up the road." Today, most of her family lives on her street and she has a network of "about two hundred people in Raleigh that are related to me." Raya's experience is in line with scholarship observing that conformity within the diaspora to traditional ethnic values and roles requires familial integration into an ethnic community that fosters this socialization (Haller & Landolt, 2005; Langfield, 2009; Zhou, 1997). This social setting partially explains how Raya and other second generation Palestinians have become closely tied to homeland conflict, especially as compared to second generation Jewish Israelis, as we will see later on in the chapter.

Raya is very active in both ethnic and religious associations, unlike other second generation respondents. She is a member of several Muslim, Arab, and even Jewish organizations on her college campus. Not surprisingly, as Raya was raised with and has preserved a strong Palestinian and Muslim identity, she is well-informed about the conflict. Her U.S. family speaks with contacts in Palestine and passes on the information to her; this is her primary means of keeping up to date, but she also reads *The New York Times* and Yahoo News as well as watching Al Jazeera and following an Israeli source, *The Jerusalem Post*, to get other perspectives. For her part, Naimah feels more informed now than she did in the past, which she attributes to starting college: "I just feel a little more than I did before, just because I was so detached before. But now I'm actually like learning more, talking to more people." Similarly, Raya told me that upon starting high school—the first diverse and public school she had ever attended—her understanding of the conflict transformed. She began to make concerted efforts to learn about both sides of the conflict:

> And I tell my parents all the time that I really didn't believe that a two-state solution was possible until I entered my world civilizations class in sophomore year in high school. And I was that kid—I would cross out the word "Israel" and write in "Palestine" and that's it. And I would get into debates where

> it was me versus everyone else in that room. But then I started really understanding and seeing, and I was like, you know, really there's innocent people on both sides and you can't really categorize innocent people. And I just think with Palestinians and Israeli people, it just cuts out the work to break things down into good and evil, and black and white.

Raya has continued her efforts to learn more about the conflict, mainly by discussing it with various people in the United States who have divergent opinions. She considers the media coverage unsatisfactory because it glosses over the conflict—"It just doesn't have all the history in it"—and can be confusing to outsiders. She also thinks that American media portray Israelis in a more positive light than Palestinians, but blames this partly on Palestinians themselves, who do not lobby for their rights as much as Israelis:

> I feel like the Palestinians have had to fight more to be like, this is what's really happening. I think to a certain extent, though, that it's the fault of the Palestinian Americans, because we're the ones who can influence the media and we can write letters to magazines. You know, I subscribe to *The Jerusalem Post*... and they were in an outrage over Jimmy Carter's book [probably 2006's *Palestine: Peace Not Apartheid*] and they were like, you need to send letters. As Palestinians we don't try to change the bias, so I mean, if you don't try to change it then you deserve, I think, every bit of what happens to you.

Naimah also shared the hostile-media perception, believing that media in the United States support Israel and represent Arabs as prone to violence. She thinks that "maybe [Arabs] are portrayed that way in the current media because of the Israel backing by the United States." Josef spoke specifically about media-derived perceptions of Palestinians: "When you say 'Palestinian' nowadays, most people think terrorist rather than thinking about a group of people, or a people without a country." Yasir expressed similar opinions on media bias and the greater success of the Jewish Israeli American community in being heard; what is distinct in his framing is his reliance on Jewish stereotypes: "The media is controlled by many powerful Jewish people. The Israeli lobby, the Jewish lobby in the White House, is very powerful. Money in this country talks." In an exchange that highlighted my own positionality as a Jewish American researcher—but that also showed remarkable candor on Yasir's part—he continued:

> *Yasir*: Every time one Jewish person dies, it's on the news. Our kids, they die left and right, and you don't hear about it in the media. It's pro-Jewish, pro-Israeli media. They are very powerful.
>
> *Interviewer*: The media or the Jewish people?
>
> *Yasir*: They are influenced by the Jewish lobby. Right? You said you won't be offended, right? I'm just telling you the way it is.
>
> *Interviewer:* No, not at all. I want to know what you think.

Yasir also commented on the effects of media bias and skewed reporting which encourage the classification of Palestinians as terrorists:

> It makes it to somebody who's not with our side, they listen and say, these Palestinians are thugs, killers, and the poor Jewish people, they defend themselves. And this is the way it is. The guys with the tanks and M-16s and the guy with the handmade gun are equal? This guy's shooting with a little gun, and this guy hit him with the M-16s? Who's coming to whose house? Who is being mistreated? Who is suffering day and night? Some parts of Israel, most of Israel, they live like this—a very peaceful life, they don't know anything. But all Palestinians under occupation live horribly.

Yasir uses a wide range of media, including CNN and Al Jazeera on television and various internet sites. He watches CNN and Fox because, "I like to see what these right wings say, what hatred comes out of their mouths." Burhan similarly noted that he will sometimes actively turn to media outlets from which he expects bias:

> Primarily Al Jazeera is the main channel that I watch. I always flip immediately—when I hear a report, I immediately flip over to CNN or Fox. I want to see from what angle they

> are reporting any story. When it comes to the Palestinian issue, it's not reported unless it is a suicide attack or there's a major military operation that's going on. Day-to-day suffering of the people themselves are only reported by the Al Jazeera and documentary movies.

Asim and Ahmed's main source of information is the BBC because, as Asim put it, "I find it the most medium [i.e., moderate]. They're not all Arabs, so they're not Al Jazeera, and they're not pro-American, like Fox or CNN." Asim also relies on emails from his cousins in Palestine for additional details on day-to-day conflicts. Josef compared American and European media coverage, acknowledging American media tendencies towards emphasizing violence for the sake of a more sensational story:

> And when you read the American newspapers, they were talking about "terrorists" and "riots" and etcetera, and when you got *The Economist*, which is a British-based news magazine, it was ..."peaceful demonstrations"... So it was very, very different wording and that's very frustrating when I see that distinction going on.

Adara not only thinks that American media sources are biased, but, like Gameel, sees them as vapid and useless: "I'll see CNN and they devoted more time to Anna Nicole Smith's death than anything else, and meanwhile everything else that's going on in the world just doesn't get any attention." She relies upon multiple information sources, including Al Jazeera, the BBC, and personal contacts her family has in Palestine. Here she compares her own feelings about the conflict to the first generation:

> I think the first generation people, just because they could actually experience it, whereas we hear about it secondhand, so it's probably a little bit stronger for them then it would be for someone like me. I think if I were actually over there and experienced everything that happens, it would hit a lot closer to me than it does right now.

Hana also uses a variety of sources, including her parents, the BBC, CNN, and online posts and blogs. She too varies her media usage because she believes that American media are biased: "So often the American stations have a very generic, one-sided, more towards what the Israelis are doing right compared to what the Palestinians have done wrong, whereas BBC and stations like that are at least more balanced, somewhat." Hana thinks that this media bias actually further encourages both her and her father's devotion to the cause. When asked how she thinks things would differ if mainstream media favored Palestinians instead of Israelis, she had the following to say:

> Maybe, honestly, it might make me more regularly informed . . . [but] it might make me more apathetic because, like, being home with my father when he sees the news, there's so much more passion and emotion; whereas, if it's all just positive for the Palestinian then you're still supportive, but it doesn't spark something inside of you as much.

Speaking about reasons why they sometimes avoid media coverage of the homeland, respondents cited factors such as emotional distress and overload. Raya does not like to watch Al Jazeera and sometimes avoids hearing about Palestinian conflicts because knowing hurts her. Adara likewise asserted, "I tend to avoid the news because it's just so biased, but it really breaks my heart." Later in the interview she said:

> You realize that this has been going on for so long and you just grow callous to it. I don't want to say you don't care, you just kind of grow apathetic to it—where you know what's going on, but you're like, well, I can't do anything about it so why even bother thinking about it?

Ahmed similarly described his current information access:

> So I do follow [the news] but it's not as intense and devoted as I used to be, because I just got to a point where it just started to consume me for no evident reason, for no change. I'm just adding stress and anxiety to myself—why? You know, I'm not even involved in the conflict. It's just that, you know, it's not going to make a difference, unless something really severe takes place, that I would generate a response to the news.

Some of these statements are similar to ones from the first generation; however, a key difference here is that while the younger generation can, to some degree, avoid conflict-related negative emotions simply by avoiding media access, the first generation feel they can never really turn a blind eye to homeland conflict or turn off the associated pain. Because the first generation lived through the conflict, they feel obligated to continuously know what is happening to their homes and families back in Palestine. Asim noted explicitly that he feels "less likely to be emotionally deprived or distraught" because of the conflict than members of the first generation. And Hana and Naimah's words demonstrate the overall reduced salience of the conflict in the lives of the second generation: Hana commented that, "You know, when I see it on the news I think about it. I try to keep up with everything, but it's definitely not something that's always on my mind," while Naimah noted, "I don't think about [the conflict] a lot, but when I see something on TV, like, it hits me strong—anger, sympathy…" These results help verify, in congruence with assimilation and transnationalism literature, that the first generation is more homeland-oriented and emotionally impacted by events there than the second (Haller & Landolt, 2005; Levitt & Waters, 2002; Portes & Rumbaut, 2005; Zhou, 1997).

Accordingly, second generation respondents also rely less on contact with homeland friends and family for news of the conflict. Josef predominantly uses British media to find out about Middle East happenings, whereas his father talks to people in Palestine to gather information and then passes it on to Josef. Asim, like most others, has family in Palestine, but he is mainly in contact with them only during the holidays, while his mother speaks with them much more frequently. Raya, meanwhile, articulated one possible mechanism by which the existence of the conflict may work as a positive feedback loop distancing the two generations:

> I feel bad because I feel like there's this abyss between me and my relatives that live over there or that are first generation from there, because I will talk to them and it's like crickets. I'll talk to my grandma—I haven't seen her since I was nine… She doesn't like coming to America. Different things, like, I feel like to a certain extent they separate themselves from us—the second generation—because there's something about us that's different.

Since Yasir was born in Palestine and lived there for a couple of years, I asked him whether he considers himself to be first or second generation. His response articulates precisely what I see as the most important factor distinguishing the first and second generation in homeland conflict identity effects—"Second [generation], because I don't know about it. I just go by what people say about it, what's going on, seeing that injustice people suffer." For Yasir, generational status is not defined by how long one lived there but by how one connects with central homeland issues.

And yet, it is worth remembering Yasir's strongly-expressed feelings about the conflict as quoted earlier. On the one hand, then, he derives part of his self-identification ("second generation Palestinian American") from his perceived *distance* from homeland conflict, but on the other, his opinions on the issue and its portrayal in the media show that he is hardly disconnected from it. In the interviews, I asked every participant to measure, on a given scale[2], how informed they think they are about the Israeli-Palestinian conflict. Of my five first generation subjects, each claimed they gather information on a daily basis. Additionally, they consider themselves to be at the highest level offered—"totally informed"—except for Umar, who says that although he keeps up with the conflict no one can be truly informed because they are not there in the midst of it, and thus cannot get an accurate picture of what is going on. Of the nine second generation individuals, not one referred to himself or herself as "totally informed," although they were still very much engaged, as evidenced by their answers, all ranging between "somewhat informed" and "mostly informed."

FIRST GENERATION JEWISH ISRAELI AMERICANS

In comparison to Palestinians in the diaspora, for whom conflict is by far the predominant homeland concern, Jewish Israeli Americans frequently mentioned that it is crucial for them to be informed about several areas of Israeli life, including but not limited to the conflict. Members of this group's first generation, including Moshe, Ofer, Gil, Maytal, Liat, Tzipora, and Noam, noted that although the Israeli-Palestinian conflict takes precedence, it is one of many going on in Israel. According to Noam, "The internal conflicts are between

---

[2] Please see Appendix A for this scale.

orthodox and non-orthodox Jews, between Sephardic and Ashkenazi Jews. There are lots of conflicts in Israel, but I see them as secondary to conflict between Israel and the Arabs." When asked if homeland conflict is something she thinks about a lot, Liat noted, "It is, but I mean, there's also pressing issues in terms of the economy and stuff, which I didn't mention, but that's also a huge thing." Gil frequently talks to his family in Israel over the phone, and "usually when we talk, we don't talk about the [conflict] situation and so on, unless we have nothing else to talk about."

When asked at the end of our interview if he would like to add anything, Noam repeated his opinion that incessant conflict coverage overrides other highly important aspects of Israeli life:

> And so if there's anything that you can somehow add to [your study], so that to better highlight the positive aspects, not only the military aspects, the power, one of the strongest military powers in the world. I mean, that we are, but there are other things to talk about. And the willingness of Israel to compromise, the voice in the street that you hear, which is we want peace. We are willing to pay for that. Not whatever, but within reason. And the idea of a Palestinian state is in general accepted. And that's not entirely clear in the world—what really the attitude of the average Israeli is.

Several Jewish Israeli subjects took up this theme as well, discussing how U.S. media in particular exaggerate the conflict while ignoring peace-making efforts[3]. Media reflect and reinforce group-level divisions and antagonisms, an identity-related process Talbot (2008) refers to as "sociology of the enemy".

Several respondents confirmed my expectation that the first generation uses homeland connections to get conflict updates, and that they do so more frequently than the second generation. Ofer mentioned a Lebanese friend he was concerned about during the recent war with Lebanon, and his parents, who live on a kibbutz less than half a mile

---

[3]A study by Slater (2007) comparing coverage of the conflict in the *New York Times* and the Israeli *Haaretz* offered support for this sort of idea, concluding that, "The range of discourse in Israel over Israeli policies toward the Palestinians is far greater than it is in the United States concerning all the most crucial issues…" (p. 118).

from the border: "…My parents' house is one of the very last houses. I mean, I'm on the phone every day." Noting his preference for direct details over media depictions, he said, "You hear something here, but it's not necessarily correct." In addition to reading Israeli papers online and streaming Israeli radio stations, Maytal also hears from people there—"from my parents—from my mom—and from our friends." Moshe gets his information on the conflict from a wide spectrum of resources, ranging from the "internet, friends both here and there, newspaper, telephones—most of my family are there—*News and Observer* [a local U.S. newspaper]." Like Moshe, Noam relies on a broad range of local and national American media, and also reads a monthly diaspora report.

I discovered that both groups demonstrated hostile-media perception, though there was some agreement across groups on the relative biases of certain media sources; both Jewish Israeli Americans and Palestinian Americans felt that major American networks such as CNN and Fox lean more towards the Israeli side, while the BBC and other European sources support the Palestinian cause. I have already discussed Palestinians' lamentations about mass media portrayals of them as villains and aggressors. Here, we hear parallel perspectives, first with a quote from Gil about the Lebanon War in 2006, then from Noam, then Liat, and lastly from Tzipora:

> …I feel like there was a very black and white view of things sometimes. In the same way that there has to be good and evil for some people, then there has to be an assailant and a victim, and Israel was the assailant and the bad guys, and… Lebanon were the victims. I think reality is much more complicated than that . . . the BBC was very anti-Israel… (*Gil*)
>
> *Noam*: I don't agree with the media in general—the way that they're reporting about things that are happening in Israel. I think most of the media is pro-Arab and pro-Palestinian, or at least they put more weight on things that happen to the Palestinians, rather than what happens to Israelis and why. They tend to take things out of context. It was very clear during the second Israeli and Lebanon war. Only Fox news had a more balanced view. In comparison, it's more pro-Israel, so maybe there was that objective even. But in general,

> CNN and a lot of things, you can see how they… it's more, how should I say? It's more… it's more attractive for them to have things that show the poor Palestinians, how their homes were destroyed or you know, how they suffered, rather than showing what happened on the Israeli side during the bombing, even though hundreds of homes, thousands of them were bombed and killed. But the major emphasis of the media was on the Arab side.
>
> *Interviewer*: Why do you think that is?
>
> *Noam*: I think it sells better. It's more sensational. It's more appealing to feelings of people. You know, the underdog of the story.
>
> …And I think that the media was biased towards the Palestinians, and I think the media is anti-Semitic to a certain respect, and the UN is as well . . . And also I think that the media in the United States is very opinionated and the reporters express their opinion, and a lot of times the cool thing is to be with the underdog, and the underdog is the Palestinians. (*Liat*)
>
> …So the media will show what the Arab world, maybe, wants to show… It will take what some Arab leaders want to show… I don't like what the media's doing. I think the media is hurting. I think the media can play a key role in helping the process, but of course, that's not the way to make money, like a soap opera. (*Tzipora*)

Like Palestinian subjects, these individuals view mainstream media as unreliable and not to be trusted; the press constructs a distinct version of reality through culturally-framed interpretations of events (Gilens, 1999). As Moshe put it, "I think the media only chooses what will be good for the media, even if it's not true all the time." Liat thinks that "there's so much censoring going on in the U.S. that it, like, amazes me… I don't like to watch the news in general." She relies on Israeli media and her family and friends there to keep up on homeland issues. Ofer added, "…Mostly what you see on TV and hear on the radio . . . is most of the time not a reality. It's what they want to show you, like what they show you in Iraq." In his discussion of how the recent Lebanon War affected him, Gil said:

> I felt that it was very problematic in terms of knowing what's going on, because I feel like I can't really trust anyone. I don't trust the media. I don't trust Israeli media. I don't trust the international media. I definitely don't trust the Hezbollah media. So there was no…it's just like triangulating things from various places and you don't really know what's going on, and that bothered me a bit.

As a result, Gil avoids news media and relies on his family members, all of whom are still in Israel, as well as his friends here to get information about the ongoing conflict.

Tzipora also uses her transnational social network, spanning the United States, Israel, and Argentina, to gather information about Israel, as well as Israeli and Jewish local sources. When asked about her personal connections in the U.S. and Israel, Tzipora told me, "I have family in Israel. Most of my friends and everyone is connected to the issue. It's very difficult for me to be friends with somebody who doesn't care." The conflict is integral in her daily life and social relationships, as it often is for the first generation diaspora.

When asked if he ever uses Israeli residents as sources of information, Noam said:

> Not really. I find that people in Israel don't really care to talk too much about the situation. Even during the war in Lebanon our friends here, the neighbors, were there in Haifa. They have a house there. And I talked to them and they said we are visiting friends and so on. Nobody talks about the air raids. It's there, of course, and you live though it, but it's not a topic that's discussed every day. There are other things which interest Israelis just as much. I mean, it's not that security is not important, of course it is, but they don't think about it all the time. They live normal lives. So it's not a discussion topic every time they meet.

While the conflict certainly seems to loom large as a concern for many Israeli Americans, it is worth noting the contrast between Noam's generalization about Israelis in the homeland—"They live normal lives"—and the conflict-defined homeland accounts of the Palestinian respondents.

Noam brought up an interesting point also referenced by several Jewish Israelis—because he is watching the situation from the outside, he thinks he has a more objective understanding of the conflict than those directly involved:

> But if you are living abroad, listening to different news and sort of see perhaps the larger picture, though maybe not necessarily the right picture, but a different picture, I think that can all be help to give some feedback, criticism, and comments about the situation.

Rachel commented similarly on her outsider perspective. She attributes her realizations over time to accumulating varying media sources and perspectives:

> *Rachel*: Um, I think yes, living here did change it a little bit. I can see it more from the outside, more—not objectively—but more like people here see it… I can see a lot of things that are wrong in Israel in the way we do treat the others, the Arabs…
>
> *Interviewer*: What do you think helps you see things from a better perspective? Was it just being away from it, or was it having different media sources, or talking to people?
>
> *Rachel*: Media sources, yes. That's important because so much that you get is from the media, and in Israel I think it's repeating the same thing again and again. It really makes you more and more emotional and less and less rational about everything… And it's also just the experience of living in a different place and seeing Israel not as the center of the world, but maybe more in proportion.

Maytal also thinks that distancing herself from the conflict has changed her opinions about it. However, her shift was in the opposite direction from Rachel's:

> I used to be a left wing in Israel and kind of be against the war in Lebanon and be against the Palestinian occupation, and living here kind of made me look at it from a distance… I have a tendency to kind of forgive Israel for doing things because I see it from a distance and I know it's not just Israel,

> it's the Palestinians, which you don't even hear about in the news when you're there... All these countries hate Israel, so I have a tendency to kind of say, you know, you have a right to do things to survive.

Gil described how his perspectives changed over time, particularly after he emigrated from Israel:

> And I was very critical towards Israel—Israeli culture—even though that's the only culture I lived in at that point. And once I came here I started to see more positive things as well. So I'm still critical, but now I can see the good things about it. So that has changed.

Jewish Israeli Americans also cited organizations as sources of connection to the homeland and the conflict. The most popular form of organizational membership for Jewish Israeli American subjects is belonging to a synagogue, which can help them build a sense of community and connect with other Jews and Israelis as they face a much more religiously and ethnically diverse society than Israel (Gold, 2007; Rebhun & Lev Ari, 2010). Religion is a common form of transnational activism and substantially impacts identity construction (Connor, 2009; Haller & Landolt, 2005; Levitt, 2003, 2009; Levitt & Jaworsky, 2007). For Efrat, joining a religious community has helped her recapture her Israeli heritage, which she once purposefully shed:

> I would say that over the past two years I have had this amazing experience in going back to synagogue . . . Once I decided to stay in America, I think I kind of distanced myself from Israel, and I distanced myself from Israelis, and I kind of turned my back on a lot of my heritage... and I think that's begun to change. I feel more like I want to reclaim some of my identity and my heritage.

Noam and several others are members of both temples and Jewish organizations that give large sums of money to Israel. Tzipora is a member of several of these associations and works for one of them. She told me about a particular organization dedicated solely to "Israel advocacy for the media and explaining, behind the scenes, what's happening."

Remarking on generational discrepancies, Noam made the following comparisons between his three sons and himself:

> I think that the older ones have strong feelings towards Israel. They are not the types who really don't care, but I don't think that they read much about it. If they know something about it, it's never going out of their way to find interesting resources for the information. They probably hear what they hear on CNN, I would say, the sort of typical coverage. They are not going to any blogs. They are not going out of their way to get diverse opinions or analyze and research the situation.

Tzipora drew similar conclusions in comparing first and second generation Jewish Israeli Americans: "The problem is if you care as much. And I'm not sure, I don't think that you care as much, especially if you live in a country where you're comfortable and free, and you forget about how connected your reality is to what's happening around the world." Gil is more connected to the conflict than those born in America who do not have family in Israel "because I have people who are important to me over there. And I am directly influenced." Maytal also expressed how it is more personal for her than for second generation Israeli Americans. "…I don't think they have the worry I have. I have an instant worry—oh, my sister's taking that bus, oh, where's my brother today?"

Prominent immigration scholars (Levitt, 2009; Levitt & Jaworsky, 2007; Levitt & Waters, 2002; Portes et al., 2009; Portes & Rumbaut, 2005, 2006; Zhou, 1997) have theorized that identities of the second generation are heavily shaped by their American upbringing, as compared to their parents' greater homeland orientation. Moshe agrees:

> …I think the way of thinking is different, because they never lived there and they don't know how it is living there and what's happening, and it's different. I will tell you, I am Israeli and they are American. It's always a big difference.

Ofer adds:

> When you're born there you are much more tied to the land, to the place. I know for my kids, I mean, as much as I try to explain to them, still they feel like for themselves they are American. And I try to speak Hebrew to them most of the time, and they don't answer much in Hebrew.

SECOND GENERATION JEWISH ISRAELI AMERICANS

First generation Jewish Israelis explained that although the conflict is the main homeland issue for them, it is not the only one that matters, nor is it an all-consuming part of daily life in Israel. Second generation responses, such as this one by Dalia, reflect these perspectives:

> It's really scary for me, like having relatives that live there and like have almost been directly affected. As far as like specific issues, like I said, I'm not on top of things, just like security in general. I mean, it's pretty safe. I never feel uncomfortable when I am there, but at the same time things have kind of hit close to home. Like when my cousin wanted to go to this disco and her mom wouldn't let her, and like that night there was a suicide bombing. You know, like that's scary, even though I've never felt uncomfortable when I was there.

Leah repeatedly mentioned that her parents taught her the importance of not allowing the conflict to intimidate her while there or stop her from going about her regular routine: "Well, I just hear lots of people say like, oh, it's not a safe time to go right now or whatever, but most of my family lives in Tel Aviv and it's not like that." Zev felt very safe living in Israel and believes that people simply have to adjust their lifestyle around the current state of the conflict, rather than allowing it to monopolize their daily lives.

As mentioned earlier, Sasha finds it frightening how people in Israel grow accustomed to bomb threats and explosions. She said she feels continuously connected because her mother and sister are still in Israel, and yet she does not see the conflict as shaping how she thinks of herself in any way. And despite her retrospective realization that she probably lived at a certain baseline level of fear in Israel, she gently mocked the mass stereotypes about life in Israel she heard from Americans who found out she had lived there: "...They're like, 'Were there always bombs exploding over there?' Or the really uninformed people—'Oh wow, did you ride a camel to school?'"

In second generation perspectives on mainstream American media and their representations of the conflict, we again see the hostile-media tendencies to view one's own people as treated unfairly, while the Other is perceived as receiving preferential treatment. Dalia illustrates this outlook:

> I think also, like, there's a lot of negative media coverage of Israel here in the U.S. and that's something that bothers me too, because I think a lot of things aren't fairly reported... Like headlines, like, oh, "Ten Killed in Israeli Air Raid," and they talk about the Palestinian babies that died or whatever, but there's no mention of the fact that ten Israeli children were killed the day before. No mention at all, or like, they'll gloss over it. Or like, let's say for example with suicide bombers, making them out to be more martyrs and talk about their family and how their family has been affected by this, and why they think he did it. Like, oh, we had no food. I don't know, like, but they don't focus on the people who were killed, especially if there's any children killed, they usually just gloss over that, I feel.

Leah sees the press as sympathetic to the Palestinian cause, and argues that such media portrayals affect the way Americans (including her) view the conflict in Israel.

> *Leah*: I think that American media tends to, they tend to focus a lot from the perspective of Israel being... I mean it's not 100% this way, but I feel like if there's going to be a touching story about the family that suffered because of the conflict, it's usually going to be like a Palestinian family. And it's not 100% but it's, say, the majority of the time. So when it's framed that way, then if it's a conflict, then the people who are creating the trouble for the family is going to be the other side, which is the Israeli side. I mean there's still a lot of focus on the suicide bombers and stuff like that, but I don't think that there are the stories about, like, some Israeli who was maimed

> because of a suicide bomber, or the family of the guy who died because of a suicide bomber. I definitely think that the American media does shape the way that Americans in general, and probably myself, think about the Arab-Israeli conflict there and…
>
> *Interviewer*: How does it shape it for you?
> *Leah*: Well, it makes you empathize with the family whose apartment is getting shelled because of a conflict that they're just stuck in the middle. And I'm not saying you shouldn't empathize with them, but why should you just empathize with them? Why shouldn't you empathize with everyone whose life is ruined because of it?
>
> *Interviewer*: Does that bring up any personal feelings, any reactions that you can identify, emotions?
>
> *Leah*: I mean, I think that I'm not like a raving… a person who's just going to be, like… I mean, like, I'm not just on one side. I feel like I try to be pretty balanced about it. But I just wonder sometimes whether the balance is… like, I'm not creating that for myself, but rather the media is kind of doing it for me in some way and shaping my opinions, which obviously it's going to do, but whether it does it even more than I know it does it.
>
> *Interviewer*: So then you would say that the mass media coverage shapes the way that you understand the conflict?
>
> *Leah*: Yeah, I mean, I can think of plenty of things that aren't touched upon in the media that could be that would change the way that people view Arab-Israeli conflict there. So I think that it does.

Zev asserted that there was media bias against the Israelis during the 2006 war in Lebanon:

> I felt like there was more coverage of the Lebanese side than there was on the Israeli side. The whole world, CNN, BBC, all that. That's why it was sort of biased against Israel, because you would see all these, like, Lebanese people crying, but they don't talk about the million people who were displaced from the north to the central. We even housed a

> whole family. And they don't describe the pain. There was very few pictures of like Katyusha rockets—well, they would show Katyusha rockets falling on buildings—but they don't show people, blood, and, like, Israeli stories that much. There were obviously more Lebanese casualties because we're talking about different technology, but even despite the fact that they had more casualties I think they should show…

I did note a generational difference in the tendency to view one's own group as being treated unfairly. Compared to the first generation, who invariably claimed the media endorse the other side, several second generation Jewish Israeli Americans maintained that although the media are indeed biased towards violence overall, they do not consistently favor one group over the other. This generational distinction demonstrates that although media are powerful and shape people's perceptions and self-concepts, there is agency involved as well, since the audience actively and differentially interprets media (Siapera, 2010)—in this case, perhaps based at least partly on different background experiences with conflict. David told me, "I mean, a lot of times they're [the media] biased one way or the other. So I take it with a grain of salt." Shai and Sasha, who share this viewpoint, expressed a more neutral outlook and attribute blame to both sides for the conflict's perpetuation. Sasha said:

> I would say probably they show Israel in a better light than Palestinians more of the time, but lately though probably less, and less the more I watch. Maybe that's just because both sides are starting to fight dirty. I don't know.

Shai added:

> The mass media here in general has been extremely pro-Israeli. There is very little coverage of non-violence in the West Bank, for example…The coverage tends to focus on violent reaction from the Palestinian side. And I've seen it over and over again, that there are significant amounts of non-violence, and yet the media focuses on the violence… It makes for better pictures in many ways.

Zev, Sasha, Dalia, and David all mentioned that the main difference between them and their parents is that the first generation tends to be more pro-Israeli and less likely to empathize with the Palestinian side.

Regarding generational differences in media usage, it is apparent that the first generation consumes media more often and more broadly than the second generation. It is also clear that first generation Jewish Israelis maintain and access social networks in Israel for information more often. Dalia does not go out of her way to get information about the conflict; she says she only reads about it if it is in the headlines of *The New York Times*. She mainly relies on her mother—who is well-informed and talks to family in Israel weekly—to update her:

> It has a lot to do with the connection that my mom has. Like, she's usually the one who will tell me about it. If I'm not home she'll be like, "Oh, did you read?", and I'll go read. Like, she'll send me an email about the letter that she sent to *New York Times* about the unfair coverage, and then I want to get involved because she's involved. I mean, yeah, I guess I have relatives there, but she's the one that I see. She's the one that's most affected by it.

Like Dalia, Sasha seeks out information on Israel infrequently, as part of her weekly process of scanning news headlines. She thinks that the media tend to "always show you just the bad stuff—the fighting, the bombings, and who killed how many people here, and oh, this many children died over there." Zev rarely searches for information on the conflict:

> I mean, in a way the Palestinian-Israeli [issue] for me has just like… it's not a pertinent issue anymore because it's just happened for so long that I don't see it as a new thing that I have to tune to the TV to hear everything that's happening, because it's just the same old story over and over again.

David, who is a dentist, mainly gets his general and Israel-related news from the television in his waiting room, which is on CNN or MSNBC all day long. Otherwise he hears things from his father—first generation interviewee Noam—who David says mostly uses the internet and friends in Israel to gather conflict information. Zev's father is his main informant, as he was heavily involved in the IDF during his career and so, "He hears it straight from the military, so that's pretty much the best." Leah too said that she gets her facts

> Either from reading something on some internet newspaper or something, or talking to my parents. Although my parents will tell me some like, esoteric, weird things because like my uncle sends them newspaper clippings. So they'll tell me about, like, actual political scandals going on and stuff that wouldn't really hear in the newspapers here because they don't really care about whether, you know, the president in Israel is corrupt or something.

The most common media sources for this group are mainstream and mainly American: CNN, ABC, and NBC (online and on television), and also popular U.S. newspapers. Second generation respondents do not report using Israeli media sources often, especially as compared to their parents. Shai is an exception amongst the Jewish Israeli respondents, as he reads a vast array of media sources from all sides of the conflict. He too thinks the media do not provide an accurate picture of what is going on in the Middle East:

> I don't believe that there is a source out there which is unbiased, but one can rely on cross-correlating and using my own previously acquired knowledge too to judge and to criticize different sources. So it's a slowly accumulating, critical process, I think.

And of course, personal ties in Israel and Palestine are common sources of information for this internationally-networked individual: "And if I happen to know who were on the ground there, I'll email them or phone them and see if I can get firsthand reports of what's actually happening."

For the most part, these members of the second generation are not heavily involved in organizations linked to being either Jewish or Israeli. Their most common association is the same as their parents—the synagogue—and even then only a few times a year, on High Holidays. The notable anomaly here again is Shai, who has dedicated much of his time to conflict resolution. He is an active member of at least three national and international organizations promoting peace in

Israel/Palestine, and he is involved with all of them on a daily basis. Shai has

> a lot of other things to do but I'm very much involved, and I see myself as very much obsessed with the conflict, and I find it very difficult to extricate myself on a day-to-day basis from what's going on over there.

Clearly, the conflict immensely impacts Shai and his self-concepts and worldview. Other second generation Jewish Israeli Americans largely demonstrate, once again, support for the notion that the conflict has less of an overall impact on them.

Leah said that when she hears about conflict in Israel:

> I mean, I guess it makes me upset a little bit but… I don't know, for good or bad I'm kind of busy with other things, so it doesn't really affect my life too much . . . Your life must go on, so it's not necessarily affected by what's going on in the news.

When asked about how the conflict affects her, Dalia said:

> If I hear about it, it affects me, but the problem is that I'm kind of in my own little bubble. I don't know, it doesn't affect me any more than anything that happens here affects me… It's just something that happens in your life, or like, it's something that you read about and you're like, that sucks, I wish there was something I could do, but at this point in my life there's nothing I can do. And then I just kind of move on, I guess.

She went on to more specifically address the question of her emotional reactions to the conflict: "It's more like sometimes I see my mom really upset because she has all the connections, and then that upsets me. But I directly don't really get very upset." When asked about the differential impact of hearing about conflict, David said his father (Noam) is much more vocal about it, and that, "obviously it hits home more to him because he was born there."

It is telling to return to the self-reported scales on media access and compare responses across Jewish Israeli American generations. Of the eight first generation respondents, three said they are informed about homeland conflict on a daily basis, four responded that the figure is once or twice a week, and one person is informed about every two weeks. In comparison, only Shai gets news on the conflict every day, two second generation subjects are informed about once a week, and three estimated the figure as once a month or so. When asked to locate themselves on a scale of how informed they typically are about the conflict, one first generation individual said "totally informed," four said "mostly informed," and three responded "somewhat informed." As for the second generation, three claimed to be "mostly informed," one responded "somewhat informed," and two said "somewhat uninformed." There was a slight tendency overall for the first generation to get more news more often; however, as noted, the greater and arguably more interesting discrepancy arose in comparing Palestinian Americans and Jewish Israeli Americans.

CONCLUSIONS

Members of both generations and ethnic groups have an interest in keeping up to date, but there are group-level differences in how they access and are influenced by conflict information. While first generation respondents rely on a combination of personal networks and both homeland-based and national and international media sources, the second generation predominantly uses their parents and American news sources for information. As well, as I had anticipated, the first generation more frequently access and are more emotionally impacted by reports on the conflict than are their children. But the second generation, despite overall lower levels of perceived involvement in the conflict and of staying informed on it, still consistently displayed some degree of identification with the group in relation to homeland conflict issues.

Both groups and generations showed distinct hostile-media perceptions, with respondents believing that mainstream media were biased in favor of the other group. Notably, several Palestinian American respondents reported purposely seeking out media with viewpoints that differed from or were even opposed to their own, in order to gain a broader perspective or better understand how the other side frames its arguments. Jewish Israeli Americans did not remark on such a tendency in their own media use.

Palestinian Americans as a whole are to some degree more aware of and burdened by the conflict, as it is an ever-present concern for their friends and family living in Palestine; on the other hand, Jewish Israeli American respondents felt able to make statements such as "They live normal lives" in reference to homeland contacts. As discussed, all but one first generation Palestinian American identified themselves as "informed daily" and "totally informed," while only three out of nine first generation Jewish Israelis get news on a daily basis, and just one felt "totally informed." And the range of how informed they are is much higher overall for both generations in the Palestinian population than the Jewish Israeli group. Despite this ethnic group differentiation, I observed, via their reports on information sources, an overall tendency in both groups toward at least some level of ongoing emotional investment in conflict in their shared homeland.

CHAPTER 4:

Experiences in the Host Country

Following from the previous chapter's exploration of how information on homeland conflict is accessed from the host country, the central question of this chapter is how the general experience of living in the United States impacts Palestinians' and Jewish Israelis' diasporic identities in relation to the ongoing conflict. Before analyzing subjects' identity processes at the individual level, it is first imperative to investigate macro-level conditions, such as historical precedents, since host and home country dynamics matter (Rumbaut, 2002). Worldwide reactions (including the United States') to Jewish and Palestinian discrimination and persecution have greatly differed (Dunsky, 2008; Ellis, 2002; Khalidi, 1997; Said, 1979). Zionist nationalist efforts after the Holocaust were successful, while Palestinian calls for a nation of their own have been largely ignored in the past (Chomsky, 2010; Khalidi, 1997). Israel receives \$3 billion in foreign economic and military aid each year from the United States (Patterson, 2006) and between 1949 and today, the total amount received is over \$100 billion (Dunsky, 2008). These numbers are authenticated by the Congressional Research Service report (Sharp, 2010), which further notes that Israel is the largest cumulative recipient of U.S. aid since WWII. Palestinians have received far less economic support, and many argue that they have gotten far less political support as well (e.g., Chomsky, 2010; Dunsky, 2008; Ellis, 2009). These factors in turn affect the rights and livelihood of individuals living in both the homeland and the diaspora. Such inequalities also shape diasporic identity, since identity is in part politically-determined; power and exclusion play a key role in identity processes (Georgiou, 2006).

This chapter particularly examines respondents' experiences in the United States in the critical area of perceived reception or rejection. I explore ethnic group and generational differences in encountering ethnic discrimination in the U.S. as well as perspectives on the host country's historical and current role in the Israeli-Palestinian conflict. These areas are important to explore since minority group identities are partially shaped—and can even be imposed—by dominant characterizations of the group and by their given social status (Gans, 2007; Zimmerman et al., 2007).

I hypothesized that Palestinian subjects would relay more individual-level incidents of discrimination and express more institutional-level dissatisfaction regarding America's involvement in the Israeli-Palestinian conflict. The first expectation, that Palestinians would cite a greater number of interpersonal confrontations, is based on the previously-mentioned violent portrayal of Arabs in the press and mainstream multimedia (Marvasti & McKinney, 2004; Noakes & Wilkins, 2002; Siapera, 2010). Palestinians and Arabs face stigmatization and stereotyping in the United States, especially since the events of September 11th, 2001 (Cainkar, 2009; El-Aswad, 2006; Marvasti & McKinney, 2004; Noakes & Wilkins, 2002). Jews in America were regular victims of ethnic discrimination in pre-industrialized America and for several decades thereafter, but since World War II, prominent anti-Semitism has largely abated (Brodkin, 1998).

My second expectation, that Palestinians would convey frustration with America's role in the conflict, is founded on claims that the U.S. has actively supported the Zionist movement and financially backed Israeli military incursions into the occupied territories (Chomsky, 2010; Dunsky, 2008; Ellis, 2009; Patterson, 2006). Certainly, the Jewish American diaspora has successfully developed immense support for Israel and Zionism through their powerful and well-organized nonprofit and advocacy institutions (Gold, 2007; Patterson, 2006; Rebhun & Lev Ari, 2010). Two examples of powerful Jewish American groups are the Conference of Presidents, where leaders of large Jewish organizations collaborate and work with the executive branch of the United States' government; and AIPAC, which works with Congress to alert elected representatives to Israel's needs and financially supports congressional candidates who advocate for Israel (Patterson, 2006, p. 1899).

Differences in organizational and lobbying efficacy matter for economic prosperity and also for basic survival. It has been theorized that without the United States' financial, military, and intelligence assistance, Israel might have ceased to exist long ago (Patterson, 2006; Said, 1979; Shain, 1996). It is also argued that without the Jewish diaspora's successful mobilization efforts and organizational wealth, American aid to Israel would not have been so readily available (Patterson, 2006). Some Israeli American subjects, including Gil and Zev, mentioned that although they are grateful for U.S. aid to Israel, they also think this relationship involves perceptible (and somewhat begrudged) power inequalities—the United States feels entitled to a say in Israeli military action. U.S. fiscal and military support for Israel causes considerably greater discomfort for Palestinian American subjects, who resent having to pay tax dollars to, as they see it, fund the occupation and oppression of their people in Palestine.

FIRST GENERATION JEWISH ISRAELI AMERICANS

Typically, the longer these immigrants stay in the U.S., the more they come to see America as their home (Rebhun & Lev Ari, 2010). Sixty-four-year-old Noam moved to the United States at the age of twenty-five and has lived all over the country. When asked if he would ever consider moving back to Israel, he said it was "not very likely. We are so settled here and we have our three boys here." He later noted that he thought it would be interesting for my study to compare more recent immigrants' homeland attachments and plans to return with his own feelings as someone who has lived in the U.S. for almost forty years. Ofer, who has lived in America for over twenty years, also alluded to this idea of looking for longitudinal changes in identity. When I asked him if he sees Israel as his homeland, he paused and replied, "Yes, but if you asked me this question fifteen years ago I would say much more so. Now it's like this is my home . . . [but] Israel is my homeland…" Asked about his long-term views on the conflict, he responded:

> Israel didn't change. I felt more Israeli then, and now this is my home. That's really the only difference. I've lived in Raleigh almost eleven years, so this is definitely my home, but my view about the conflict, that's definitely not going to change.

As I will demonstrate, consistent with scholarship such as Waldorf's (1995) study that found time in the host country to be a significant factor in return-migration intentions, more recent émigrés express more of an immediate and concrete desire to move back, as their family ties and homeland memories are still very salient. They also visit more often and maintain more comprehensive, concentrated social networks there.

Although Noam does feel that America is his home, he also discussed how growing up in Israel forever altered his self-concept and outlook:

> Well, you know, when you are born in Israel and raised in Israel for twenty-five years, your loyalty and your feelings towards the country, especially since I served in the military and went into reserves, I feel very strongly connected to the country. So even though I lived in Europe and am living in the United States for many years, I still feel deep inside as an Israeli, and I see everything from an Israeli perspective. But I can also see it from an American perspective, a Western perspective.

This statement reflects the complexity involved in transnational identities—one can simultaneously feel attached to both home and host country (Gans, 2007; Haller & Landolt, 2005; Levitt & Waters, 2002; Portes & Rumbaut, 2006; Wald, 2009; Waters & Ueda, 2007; Zimmermann et al., 2007). Increasingly, studies on transnationalism are stressing the synergistic relationship between assimilation and transnational practices (Levitt & Waters, 2002, p. 5).

According to Noam, his continual Israeli perspective on life distinguishes him from his sons, who were raised in America and thus see things from a different cultural standpoint. Moshe's identification with Israel is similar to Noam's but more exclusive. When asked what he identifies as, he said, "I am Israeli. I'm American, but no, I'm Israeli. I was born Israeli and I will die Israeli. No matter how many years I live in America, I will always be Israeli. It's in my blood." In comparison, he explained that while he will always be Israeli, his children are definitely American, even though they also have Israeli passports.

Noam mentioned how he has consistently felt a desire to be back in Israel for, at the very least, extended periods of time. Other first generation respondents also stated that the pull to return never subsides, and that this sets them apart from their children, for whom America is the only home they know or need. Rachel said:

> Well, we do feel so much like part of Israel. I think that will probably never change . . . It's still very basic to both of us [her and her husband], this feeling that we're Israeli and we need to be in Israel. So everything that happens really affects us.

When Efrat decided to stay in America she felt "initially a little twinge of guilt about staying in the United States because . . . I felt very proud as an Israeli and didn't want to be known as a *yoredet*." The term *yored* is a pejorative referring to an Israeli who emigrates. Socialization in Israel heavily emphasizes that Jews should live in Israel; thus, this term reinforces the preservation of transnational identities by inducing guilt and intentions to return (Cohen & Gold, 1996; Gold, 2007; Rebhun and Lev Ari, 2010). This particular stigma has waned over time as Jews and Israelis in the diaspora, especially in the U.S., have come to be recognized as playing a very important role in protecting and supporting Israel (Gold, 2007; Rebhun & Lev Ari, 2010). Moshe's "dream is to live part of the year in America and part of the year in Israel. Only if my kids decide to do aliyah [move to Israel and become Israeli citizens] it would be wonderful!"

As Maytal, who moved here about five years ago, put it,

> Sometimes I would hear Israelis that come here say we don't even intend to go back, and that kind of highlights even more to me that I'm an Israeli… I feel like maybe Israel is not doing always the right thing but that's my land. You know, I am going to go back there and change it if possible.

She said she does not belong anywhere among various groups in America and always feels like an Israeli outsider, which increases her wish to return. When it comes to her children, though, she said, "…they're Americans. They don't want to hear about us going back." Maytal and Liat, despite expressing desire to move back, invoked the specter of the conflict when they described how living in America has been a reprieve from their stressful homeland lives. Liat, who had moved back to America just a year before our interview, said, "But now that I am here I also was, like, relieved that I don't have to deal with the tension, because if I was in Israel I would not feel safe."

Noam, Tzipora, and several others are active members of Jewish American transnational organizations. Their discussions exemplify the extensive and powerful connections the Jewish American diaspora helps maintain between Israel and America (Rebhun & Lev Ari, 2010). As Noam put it, "We, the diaspora, need Israel, as Jews, and Israeli Jews need American Jewry's support." Liat added:

> I think the United States is supportive of Israel… Part of that is the relationship that American Jewry has with, I guess, American politicians. So there is an influence of the rich Jews to a certain extent on policy… It makes me feel secure as an Israeli to know that the Jews are watching out for us… at least in America.

Tzipora, Moshe, Ofer, and Efrat discussed how they were not very religious in Israel and did not feel that they had to be, because their Jewish identity was reinforced by their community and schooling, whereas in the diverse setting of the United States there is a greater need to seek out support for this identity. A related factor is the distinct religious-secular divide in Israel. Ofer, like most Israelis, was raised celebrating the Jewish holidays and studying the Torah in school, but he was not brought up with a religious identity like the one he now encourages for his own children. Ofer's wife—who was present during our interview—described this dichotomy:

> There are just many people in Israel who are offended by the sort of stated theocracy, and so they become anti-organized religion. And that is completely political and has nothing to do with religion. And so while his parents are anti-religion and are really headstrong opposed to some of the practices, they raise [their children to follow] other aspects of it.

Tzipora described her Jewish lifestyle here:

> I am affiliated with the conservative synagogue but I am more a cultural Jew in many ways. It's a very strong identity as an Israeli. Only when I am in the diaspora, living outside of

> Israel, is when I need to try harder to do it for my kids, for their identity.

As mentioned earlier, Efrat discussed how with age she feels "more like I want to reclaim some of my identity and my heritage." As for joining her local synagogue, she added, "I just felt like I wanted to be more part of the community and this was a way to do that." Liat, like many others, believes that although being connected to Jewish Americans helps, "…even living in this area where there aren't a lot of Jews[1], having Israel makes me feel more secure in my identity."

Moshe added, "In Israel you don't go to Hebrew school, Sunday school. It's not part of your life like in America." He also told me how, "I have non-Jewish friends, but my closest friends are almost all Jewish." This was a recurrent comment, as Israelis' concept of kinship in the diaspora necessarily expanded to include Jewish Americans as well as Israeli Americans. This is because these relatively small American subgroups are linked by their shared religion, collective memories, and cultural practices (Mannheim, 1952). Haller and Landolt (2005) described transnational social fields as creating novel opportunities for social engagement and group construction; belonging can be redefined once it transcends a single location.

Several respondents acknowledged that America has been for the most part supportive of Israel, although some noted a recent tendency to empathize with the "underdog" (as they put it in Chapter Two) and favor Palestinian rights. First Moshe, then Liat, and finally Noam describe the former perspective:

> …I am really happy that America tried to help Israel, because America is a big country and Israel is small. And I guess that the American government sees that Israel is overall a good thing to happen, so they try to help us. Like, what happened

[1] An estimate from the Association of Religion Data Archives puts the Jewish makeup of the Research Triangle region in the year 2000 at 0.8 percent. In comparison, the adherence rate for the overall United States is estimated at 2.1 percent. These numbers may be somewhat low considering that they track regular attendees of religious services and not necessarily those who consider themselves culturally Jewish. The Muslim estimate for the Triangle region is 0.4 percent, in comparison with a national Muslim adherence estimate of 0.5 percent.

> three months ago, when Israel attacked the Lebanese, before the war. So the government of America was actually behind Israel. It was good in a way. So overall I am happy that America tries to help Israel in any way they can. (*Moshe*)
>
> ...Well, I appreciate the American involvement. I appreciate the money that America's sending over and the international support. I am proud to be American, I am proud to be Israeli, and part of that is the connection allows me to be proud of both. Because if they were in conflict I wouldn't be able to be both. So the support that America is giving and the appreciation that Israel has for America influences my identity. (*Liat*)
>
> ...I think that the relationships have been very close relationships between the two countries. And that makes me feel good to live in a country where the host government or the local government is by and large pro-Israel . . . I think that for a Jew outside of Israel this is probably the best place to live. (*Noam*)

Tzipora agreed that America and Israel are the only safe places for Jews in today's world, especially when compared with her own experiences in Argentina:

> People won't walk through a Jewish building [in Argentina] because it's a target. And I won't let my kids go with a big *Magen David* [Jewish star] on the street. You can do it here. I know that here I go to the grocery store and they tell me do you want it wrapped for Christmas or Hanukkah? . . . It's not anywhere around the world like that, unless you're in Israel.

While Tzipora acknowledged America's aid to Israel and thinks the U.S. is "the only country taking a brave step and speaking up to, 'Hey, there's something happening and we need to stop,'" she also thinks there is a tendency for people here to empathize with suicide bombers, and this bothers her greatly. She said:

> And I am also concerned as a mother because I don't like the values that the world is teaching my kids. Somehow if you do something bad we will listen to you, so if you kill yourself we

> will feel sorry for you and we will listen to you. And that's scary.

Liat thinks that the media make Palestinians out to be the victim, and "that's also maybe part of the reason that the really liberal Jews are like more pro-Palestinian than pro-Israel, because the Palestinians are the underdog, you know, we need to care for the poor people."

Nevertheless, the backing of the U.S. is greatly valued by respondents. Gil believes that, "Israel with American support and Israel without are two very different things. I don't know if Israel would even exist without American support." He thinks that if he were to live elsewhere, say in Europe, he "might have encountered considerably more situations where it would feel uncomfortable to say I'm from Israel."

While Jewish Israeli subjects mostly reported positive reception and treatment in the United States, some had experienced anti-Semitism. As I discussed in Chapter Two, Maytal has overheard discriminatory jokes and comments being made about Jews. Coworkers joked with her when she made mistakes at work about how, "it's because you're Jewish—nothing ever works for you." Or they would use terms like "Oh, you were 'Jewing' us." Efrat lived in a Jewish neighborhood of Pittsburgh for a few years as a child, and yet still, because of her Israeli/immigrant status, "it always made me acutely conscious of being in the minority . . . I was different from most of my classmates." As an adult she had only a few brushes with discrimination, such as being called names like "filthy Jew."

When discussing encounters in the United States with the Other involved in the conflict—Palestinians—respondents reported mixed feelings about how these encounters influence their Jewish Israeli identities and perspectives on the conflict. For Liat, the key global-level division is between Jews and Muslims, and she sees little room for overlap between these opposing groups:

> My first divide is Muslim, if you're Muslim or not, and if you're Muslim then I'm like fearful and more cautious. If you're not Muslim then I look to see, are you of Arab relations—so Arab, Palestinian, even Turkish, because they fall under the Muslim. And I'm threatened and cautious of those groups. I don't know if I could be friends with people of

> those backgrounds just because of the different basic world views that we have. I've worked with people like Christian Palestinians and stuff like that, but no friendship formed, probably because we're both so different on basic levels.

Some respondents, such as Tzipora, demonstrated support for theoretical assertions that this conflict is a dialectical process involving total negation of the other side (Gur-Ze'ev & Pappé, 2003; Shamir & Sagiv-Schifter, 2006). In her opinion, the following story shows how the antagonism transcends the conflict site. She made a friend from Lebanon in the United States and started teaching her Hebrew. They exchanged ethnic food recipes. Then,

> one day she told her parents that she became good friends with an Israeli, and they told her to stop it right now or we're bringing you back home, this person is dangerous. And she told her friends from her community, and they said, we don't want you to see her because we are going to do something really bad to her if we see you with her. That was the point where she said, "I can't see you anymore." And again, we're here in a different place. There is a lot of judgment. There is a lot of prejudice. It's polarized.

Maytal described the more common trend of avoiding interactions with Palestinians and Arabs in the United States in order to evade negative encounters related to homeland conflict. When asked about her perception of Palestinians, she had the following to say:

> I don't think we have any that we know. If we go to a Mediterranean place we usually try not to talk in Hebrew and not show too much that we are Israelis, because I think still even here the fear of "What if they know?" or "What would they think about us?" . . . They hate us, of course, so I think that also kind of sheds light on, "Oh, we're still Israelis" even if we don't want to be related.

Gil, when asked about his impressions of ethnic group differences, said, "Um, I don't really see or interact with Palestinian Americans. I don't know anyone." These statements align with those discussed in Chapter Two, concerning encounters with the Other in the homeland. Israeli subjects have had very limited and sporadic interactions with Palestinians throughout their lives.

In contrast to Maytal, Rachel thinks that she and Palestinians "...probably have a lot in common. We just go to a Mediterranean store and meet some Palestinians; sometimes it feels like, oh, they're from home." She was shocked to learn that many Americans categorize her as Mediterranean, thus lumping her into the same group as Palestinians. In reference to a comment made at a seminar she attended, which she found to be racist, Rachel continued:

> And so it took me a few days to realize that part of why I was offended was also because he put me in the same group as Arabs, which I wasn't used to thinking of myself in that way.

As for their overall feelings about the conflict and its resolution, most Jewish Israelis empathized with the Palestinians and said they want to see peace and national rights for both groups, while also expressing frustration with what they perceive as terrorist methods used by Palestinians. As Maytal stated, "So I do see the Palestinians as people and their suffering hurts me, but I just can't figure out why they keep fighting the way they do."

SECOND GENERATION JEWISH ISRAELI AMERICANS

When asked about which homeland issues are important to him, David first listed peace with the Palestinians, then relations between Israel and the United States. He said:

> Well, hopefully they're good [U.S.-Israeli relations], and hopefully that bond stays strong and that trust is still there and the politicians here still view Israel as an ally, that kind of thing. And back Israel in what they do—so those are things that are important.

Leah's similar comments reference the Jewish American community's crucial role in preserving and sustaining Israeli-American affairs:

> *Interviewer*: Do you feel that the United States has been supportive of Palestinians and/or Israelis?

> *Leah*: I think probably more supportive of Israelis, just because there's more… like Jewish lobby is bigger and has more money and stuff like that. And there's also more… I mean even beyond that it's the idea…like especially nowadays with, like, America's against terrorism but Israel is a democracy and historically… I guess now things are changing a little bit, but was the only democracy in the Middle East. So America's always been with Israel and on Israel's side, and now that the Palestinian government is controlled by Hamas it's… so I don't think America is really going to be supporting them.

Leah later pondered how America's unrelenting support of Israel may be tied to Christianity—a topic mentioned only by her and Zev among the Jewish subjects, but frequently discussed by Palestinian respondents, as I will show:

> Like the whole Christians who are pro-Israel, there's always this undertone that they're pro-Israel because of Christianity. When Jesus comes back, the Jews have to be there—this whole thing like we're being used or something. I'm sorry, I can't think that [President] Bush is good for Israel because of his religious perspective if he's just using us. That doesn't feel right.

Zev is pleased that there are strong bonds between the IDF and United States military:

> There's sort of a link here between the Israeli and American army. In a way, if you're like, we're the ones protecting the Western world, if you're like, we're the first offense, they're like, we have to help Israel because they're the ones who know, first of all, most about the War on Terror. We know how to fight it, we have the strategic planning and everything, and you know, that's why we're the ones helping Americans in Iraq… Also, Christians . . . for them it's important that Israel's having Jerusalem. I know American soldiers who are deployed to help in Israel, and it's just great. They send us obviously tons of, like, military weapons, and we bought

> planes from them a couple of years ago. I think the United States, for me, is the number one ally.

Zev also thinks that without American support, Israel would be obliterated:

> Like as far as [if] the United States supporting Palestine, I think Israel would have to eventually retreat. I don't think Israel would exist really. We would be fighting a lost cause, I think. Let's face it—they are a lot more than us. If they got the technology that we get then we would be off the map.

Shai agrees, but does not see the situation in a positive light akin to Zev:

> The Israeli economy and thus Israel, they couldn't exist without U.S. support, and thus the [U.S.] taxes that I pay and have to pay do go in part to fund the occupation. That's something I feel very conflicted about. I very much support the idea of stopping all U.S. tax fund aid to Israel because I believe that without the economy prop up, Israel would be forced into having a just solution to the occupation. So historically, and this has changed over time, the varying degree of U.S. support for Israel… there has been a very strong impact of U.S., especially U.S. Jewish support, which has impacted U.S. government support.

We will repeatedly see in upcoming analyses of first generation Palestinian Americans how being forced to pay money used to fund the Israeli occupation of their home causes great suffering and internal conflict.

Dalia, like many of her peers, goes to synagogue on High Holidays and feels connected to the Jewish American community, but refers to herself as "Jewish culturally, but not really religiously." Almost all second generation Jewish Israeli subjects, including Dalia, Zev, and David, only attend synagogue a few times a year, on the most important holidays. In the past, Dalia was more active in the Jewish community, participating in Jewish youth organizations. No one in this respondent group was a current member of a secular organization supporting Israel or dealing with the conflict, with the exception of Shai, who was affiliated with several international groups working to ameliorate the Palestinian situation (such as the International Solidarity Movement and the Palestine Solidarity Movement). In comparison, many first generation subjects were active members of both secular and religious ethnic organizations. Religious affiliation, like ethnicity, helps reinforce global aspects of their Jewish/Israeli identity.

As noted in the Introduction, my goal in this study is to look for prevalent trends in my sample while also acknowledging anomalous outcomes. Bonilla-Silva (2003) has suggested that a key way to overcome the potential for interviewer misinterpretation is to present "non-conforming cases" (p. 14) whenever possible. Sasha was one such case, probably the least connected respondent when it came to being Jewish and Israeli, despite the fact that she lived in Israel for several years and that her mother and sister were still there. Her ethnic and religious backgrounds are simply not important aspects of her own identity. Her social networks reflect this pattern: "I really don't know too many people who are Jewish, Palestinian, or even Israeli, anybody who has a connection to Israel, really." The only reason she is more attached to this particular conflict than any others in the world is because her family is in Israel and she is worried about their safety. Addressing why she does not maintain similar connections to the conflict as her family, she said she has always been a more independent person, and feels distant from her mother and seldom contacts her.

Shai represents the opposite end of the spectrum as compared to Sasha. Much of his daily life in the United States revolves around the conflict. He has many connections with groups in the U.S. and across the globe, and sees himself as someone bridging the gap between the adversarial groups:

> *Shai*: I've met a lot of American Jews, and American Palestinians I've been able to have very constructive dialogue with and get significantly into both the way I think and they way they think about the Israeli-Palestinian conflict. Having experienced both sides to some extent and the U.S., again I see myself as some sort of a bridge in many cases. So I have had relationships with both Jews and Palestinians here that I consider close friends and who I also consider in many ways victims of the occupation, because many of them are obsessively involved with it and are unable to proceed with

> other parts of their lives because of the continuation of the conflict and how strongly they feel connected to it.
>
> *Interviewer*: You don't see yourself as part of that at all?
>
> *Shai*: I do. I think I would much rather this wasn't going on so I could get on with other things.

Dalia made an interesting observation about changes over time in her Jewish Israeli identity. She described growing up in a little town with a small Jewish population, which encouraged her to make being Jewish her "thing":

> Like I was always like the Jewish girl and I liked teaching people about being Jewish, and then if there was ever any debate about the Israeli-Palestinian conflict I was always there. And I had like my little myths-and-facts book and I was like debating it. And I was very much more informed then than I am now.

She attributed this shift—one that moved her in the opposite direction from some respondents we heard from earlier, who felt they had become *more* knowledgeable with time—to entering a diverse college environment with a more significant Jewish population:

> I don't know, it's almost like now that it doesn't really make me different. Like, I don't see a Jewish person and get really happy because I never see Jewish people . . . And here, I don't know, maybe it's because there are so many different people, so many different ethnicities and races and just everything, that it's just not as big of a thing for me anymore.

Whereas before she had always engaged in Palestinian-Israeli conflict debates, she no longer sees the conflict as influencing her identity, other than that she is upset her to see her mother worried about it. Here we again see how the second generation's ethnic identities are largely influenced by their parents, and how the first generation tends to feel longer-lasting effects from experiencing the conflict firsthand. In contrast, their American-born children simply do not experience the same enduring ties to the homeland.

As for perceptions of the Other, Dalia drew a distinction between group cleavages in the homeland and inter-ethnic relations in the United States:

> *Interviewer*: Does the conflict make any of the boundaries/divides between different groups stronger for you?
>
> *Dalia*: In Israel I think definitely it does. Like people will look at somebody and be like, "Oh, he's Palestinian, like, stay away, he's scary." Or you know, like I wanted to go to Egypt and see the pyramids after Birthright [a program that subsidizes Jewish youths' first organized trip to Israel], and my mom was like, "No, it's dangerous, they hate Jewish people..." . . . So I think the conflict, definitely it's defined there. Here not so much. I don't know outside of [names her university] but like, here nobody really cares what you are, you know, they just accept you for who you are. There's even a group called [names the campus group], which is mainly based around just the idea that everybody should unite, but it's focused I think on the Israeli-Palestinian conflict.

Leah believed that over time, the conflict in Israel has "probably deepened [overall group] divides more." But she shared Dalia's perspective on group interactions outside of the homeland:

> I think outside of Israel...I mean, I've got friends who are Muslim, or I've worked with people who are Lebanese or from the Middle East in other places. I mean, I don't really talk with them about political issues but I think there is generally a softer attitude towards things when you're not living there. So we're able to work together and it's not a tense situation or anything—outside. But I think it's obviously tenser in Israel.

For the most part, the second generation reports the same feeling as their parents: they empathize with the Palestinian cause and want to see peace for both populations. As Zev put it, "I don't feel anger as much because I understand their point of view as well. I mean we're obviously impeding a lot of things for them as well. Just standard of living is just horrible for them."

FIRST GENERATION PALESTINIAN AMERICANS

When it comes to explaining why Palestinian subjects experience discomfort living in America, the words of the other group—Jewish Israeli Americans—perhaps build the strongest case. I asked everyone if they feel the United States supports their homeland and their side in the conflict. All of the Israeli respondents acknowledged, at least to some extent, America's historical and ongoing economic and military support of their country. In the follow-up question, I asked if they thought their relationship with the United States and the conflict would be different if the United States explicitly supported just the other side. Every Jewish Israeli subject (except for Shai) expressed that they would have a very hard time living here, and several indicated they would likely return to Israel if this were the case. Many additionally predicted that less backing by the United States government would encourage them to be more transnationally active, with the intention of gaining national support, and that it would fortify their Israeli identity.

If America was not an ally to Israel, Liat would not be able to feel proud of her dual identity as both an Israeli and an American:

> So if America was pro-Palestinian I think that I would come here, use the [graduate school] funding, and leave as fast as I can. And I would make more of a point to fight in Israel for like things that I think are important.

If this were the case, Dalia would "probably get in a lot more fights with people." Going against the mainstream, as she did back in her hometown where she was one of few Jews, would reignite her ethnic identity and connections with the conflict. Leah predicted a similar outcome: "I might be more politically active to try to change the way the U.S. government was focusing on the problem there."

Seeing how difficult it is for Israeli Americans to imagine living in the United States if the country funded Palestinian military and economic activities instead of Israeli ones perhaps make it easier to appreciate the deep-seated anguish felt by Palestinian Americans, for whom U.S. support of the opposing group in the conflict is a reality. Mansur, who had been working in the U.S. for the past thirty years, expressed feelings about being both Palestinian and American which typify the distress felt by first generation Palestinians. He thinks that,

"The United States is partners in the occupation of Palestine," and this alliance is the result of guilt about not sending troops to stop Hitler earlier in WWII. Mansur said that it seems as if anti-Semitism and criticism of Israel have become synonymous and that Americans are very careful not to "antagonize the larger Jewish community." He gave the example of Jewish American organizations' angry reaction to Jimmy Carter's use of the term "apartheid" in his recent book *Palestine: Peace Not Apartheid* (2006). For Mansur, America's unrelenting assistance to Israel is almost anti-American:

> Israel was created in 1948. The issue is simple—it was created at the expense of another people, and that's the Palestinians. That is a conflict for me. It is contradictory to the American principles, which is the right of people to be free of foreign domination and occupation, the right of people for self-determination, freedom, [to] own property, own land, or whatever they do. Well, all of these things were taken away from the Palestinians, I mean from land theft by Israel. My family lost a beautiful farm. It was taken away from us a few years ago. I consider this unbelievable. How could a human being do this to another human being? We can explain and say, well, the Palestinians are doing that and doing that, but that doesn't happen in the United States. I couldn't pass by your house and say, "That's a beautiful house," and the next day I bring my boys and four, five people armed with M-16s and machine guns and say, "We're going to take it" and they take it, it was done… I mean that's the Old West. That only would happen and it would be allowed to happen because we are the Palestinians. We are really the underdogs. We have no defenders, we have no power. We have nothing. And then they have guns and they have the United States' support, and they have the Europeans' support and the United States' military aid, economic aid, political aid, and you name it! So that's a conflict too.

He went on to explain why all of these macro-level factors matter to him personally in his own daily life:

> Another big conflict to me, and that is sort of the constant conflict, and I am sure that may be the case for many

> Palestinians in this country, which is conflict between us as Palestinian Americans who live in this country, who contribute. I know I contribute to this country, over thirty years of my youth entail the productive work at the top level of this society. And then I turn my back and I see the F-16 airplanes and our brown tanks killing civilians who are my family or my cousins. I have a conflict, here in this country I give everything to, and then this is the same country that is contributing to the suffering of my parents and my family, my brothers, my sisters. It is a conflict where I pay a lot of taxes and then I see these taxes, my own money, being used to subsidize a brutal regime against my family. When I looked at the farm we lost, it was protected by soldiers who were carrying American-made weapons, fenced by fences made in the United States, and cleared by Caterpillars made in the United States… So this is a constant internal conflict.

Safia sees the conflict between Israelis and Palestinians as so deeply entrenched and complicated, only a third party, such as the U.S., has the capacity to end it. Most Palestinians believe that their political futures will most likely be determined by external forces, the U.S. foremost among them (Bishara, 2008). Like her peers, Safia disapproves of the way the United States has mediated the peace process thus far:

> I mean, we think the key is in America's hands. And nobody is going to give up anything willingly . . . And we are in a situation where you've got two children entangled and some big, fair-minded brother or mother has to come and separate them and say, this is what has to happen. And that's not a role that the United States government is playing fairly and correctly. To me it's just very unfair.

Safia too endures significant discomfort about living in a nation that assists others in harming her family and homeland:

> I'd be so much happier living in this country knowing that my government—because this is where I will probably die, this is where I pay my taxes—was more fair-minded and more even-

> handed, and did not perpetuate the suffering of my people. I'd be much happier if people over here would be a little more aware of what's going on and not say, "Oh, if you would just stop killing Jews…", as if the whole thing is just because we're killing Jews, there's no other issue involved. It's hard to constantly be on the defense. It's hard being a Palestinian living in this country. It's very hard.

Umar views the United States' media and government as endorsing Israel and the occupation:

> I think they're not supportive of Palestinians for sure, because if they are, then they wouldn't have watched them for fifty, sixty years suffer. And are they supportive of the Israelis? I'm pretty sure they are, because that's who they give their weapons and… you know, if you support somebody with weapons against somebody else, you know that's a clear statement that I support him, not you.

When we spoke about America's support for Israel, Umar told me that he has no idea exactly why it is this way, other than it is somehow related to "personal interest of the big powers." He went on to delineate the difference between wanting America's support and wanting it to help bring an end to the warfare:

> I'm not saying, "Okay, America, you're siding with Israel, you're bad." Or, "No America, you're siding with Palestinians, you're bad." No, no, no. Don't side with nobody! Stand in the middle! Get in the middle whether they like it or not… Get in the middle, just like you get in the middle of a lot of places out there, and stop the fighting and resolve it. You're a big power!

Gameel has a similar attitude toward America's role in the conflict, and thinks that this relentless support of Israel only fuels and helps sustain the problem:

> I mean, I think it's disgraceful actually that our government here is not doing a better job of trying to resolve the conflict in

> a fair way. So it makes it hard to feel good about all the taxes one pays and everything else when they feel that.

Like Umar, Gameel does not wish the United States was pro-Palestinian instead of pro-Israel. "The thing about it is it's not about pro-this or pro-that really as much as it is about pro-making-it-work."

Safia thinks that in the long run, the United States' unwavering espousal of Israel will only lead to further destruction:

> I don't think the United States is helping Israel by perpetuating this. They may be confiscating more land but they're certainly not helping future peace. I mean, things change in hundreds of years. If things are not good for the Palestinians, also to some degree then at some point it's going to be like this mole that keeps festering and festering. And at some point the dynamics of the world powers will change and things will not be good for the Jews in that part of the world. It's much better for them to be part of that world as opposed to saying, we're Europeans, or we're this, and we're not like those people around us… Eventually they will be ejected at some point when the superpower is no longer there. Jews are safest in the United States, I believe, because they are part of the United States' fabric. They are not a separate entity and they're part of America.

She maintains that although there are many people who are supportive of both groups and seek an end to the conflict, the fair-minded voices are silenced. Jews or Israelis who are viewed as Palestinian sympathizers are treated as outcasts by those group members who are heavily invested in the conflict (Shamir & Sagiv-Schifter, 2006). Safia described her view of how anyone who criticizes Israel publicly is attacked by Israeli American advocacy and evangelical groups: "So the policy of the government is typically, basically, don't piss off AIPAC and don't piss off the Jerry Falwells or Pat Robertsons."

In Chapter One we learned that Palestinian Americans draw comparisons between Jews experiences during the Holocaust and their subsequent treatment of Palestinians. Hassan and others also compared treatment of Palestinians in Israel with African Americans' past experiences in the U.S., pointing out inconsistent implementations of American principles of equality:

> Yeah, the non-Jew, and it's like they are second class. I mean, their needs is not like your needs, you know, blah, blah, blah, so therefore no worries, don't worry… So when you strip that human element from people, then you are not going to sympathize with them… The human mind is very easy to be programmed to be honest with you… They can program it to believe that those people are worthless… They gonna look at you almost like, from here in this country, what happened to the blacks back then. People were thinking the same thing… And unfortunately that's what happened in Israel against the Palestinians. People start thinking of the Palestinians as sub-humans... That's exactly how whites used to think of the blacks—as sub-humans. So therefore, you enslave them, you kill them, you rape them, you know, and blah, blah, blah. Big deal. They're not human.

Despite Palestinian Americans' frustration with America's involvement in the Israeli-Palestinian conflict, they maintain a very strong connection to and appreciation for this country. This was especially true for first generation Palestinians who never before had a passport or a recognized home to lay claims to—neither in Palestine nor the Arab countries to which they fled after their eviction. For them, the United States fulfilled their long-standing dreams of owning a house that no one could take away, being considered equal to all others, and having civil rights. As Hassan put it:

> One thing about the Palestinian is, 'til I became a U.S. citizen, most Palestinians are stateless… It's not fun, you know, because when you are stateless, everywhere you go you are considered foreign. In Kuwait, even though it was an Arab country, we were foreign. They won't even grant you a permanent residence in Kuwait… So your movement is very limited… You know, when I became a U.S. citizen, that was the first time I ever felt like I belonged to a place.

What makes the situation even harder for Hassan is knowing that while he can never return to Israel as a citizen, "an American Jew, if they decide to go to Israel they are granted—and even though they've never seen that place before—given citizenship immediately."

In our discussion of prejudice in the United States, Umar mentioned changes in his immigrant identity and interactions over time:

> When I first came to this country I felt like a foreigner because I was new, period, regardless of where I'm from. But after living here for all these years I feel more support than I've ever felt in my life actually, recently.

When I probed him for specific examples, he spoke about the very positive community reactions he received after the collapse of the World Trade Center:

> When the September 11th took place, I was running a business here in Raleigh. I swear, I have never seen more support from local people. I couldn't believe it. People that I hadn't heard from in months were calling me to check to see if everything's okay. And that was great, absolutely magnificent.

Hassan also reported many affirming encounters with respect to his Palestinian identity in the United States. He is a member of local interfaith dialogue groups and has diverse social networks, and within both he was able to talk constructively about the events of September 11th:

> *Hassan*: Like for instance, we go get together, like I have some Jewish friends at work and some other Christians. We sit and we talk, and we say okay, we want to hash out issues and talk about problems and see… and we created a dialogue among us.
>
> *Interviewer*: Do you find that [the Palestinian-Israeli conflict] tends to be the topic of conversation, or is it just one of the many things you talk about?
>
> *Hassan*: Especially after 9/11. You see a lot of interest when it comes to the Middle East.
>
> *Interviewer*: Is there any conflict involved usually, or everyone's pretty respectful?

> *Hassan*: No, no, no. Yeah, respectful, you know, people like to know more. They ask questions of us, you know… what's going on. They start questioning, why is this happening? What do you guys stand for?

Although Hassan is able to discuss Palestinian issues within his social circles, he said that most local clubs, such as the Carolina Palestinian Club, have lost membership. When I asked him why, he said that since 9/11 people have "shied out…. A lot of them are afraid. Some of them believe in that conspiracy theory that they are going to fabricate what they say." Indeed, after the fall of the Twin Towers, many Arabs changed their names, hid their faith and kept an overall low profile in order to avoid discrimination (El-Aswad, 2006).

Mansur's post-9/11 encounters were very different from Umar and Hassan's. His exposure to discrimination impacted his identity as a Palestinian American, just as America's involvement in the conflict also influenced him:

> Our family owns restaurants, and then after September 11th suddenly there were huge rumors that we were celebrating the September 11th attacks! And you know what? We saw a very successful business, within two days nobody comes in. Zip. Business dropped 90%. And you don't think this leaves a permanent impact on me? It does. And then we got a lot of threatening phone calls in a few days after September 11th. And why? Because we are Arab American, or Palestinian American, or Muslim American. I don't know why, but it happened, and that left a permanent impact on me…

Gameel has worked on helping small groups of Palestinians, Jews, and Israelis to come together and discuss homeland concerns. Despite his willingness to speak out publicly against the occupation, he says he faces a lot of discrimination in the United States, especially since the outbreak of the Iraq War:

> It's hard not to feel discriminated against, especially in this current environment, with the war in Iraq and Arabs and Muslims, and this whole thing where people are nervous and I have an Arab name… I notice that when people see my name

> they are taken aback a little bit... And then yet there are people who are very open-minded, so I think there's both.

Safia noted that her positive interactions with Jews in the U.S. (as opposed to the consistently negative ones she had in her youth in Palestine) have helped alleviate her fear and negativity towards Israelis and Jews and instead see similarities among them:

> For me, when I see the Star of David, because it's on a lot of things that usually are oppressive for me, whether it's a checkpoint with the flag, or the soldier that's doing something to you, it has such a negative impact on me when I see it. It's a negative thing. Yet when I did work with [a local Jewish group advocating for peace in the conflict] and I'm with them in the same demonstrations, I see these wonderful ladies that I completely agree with on everything else and I love them to death, and they're wearing the Star of David. And all of the sudden it means something different to me. It's kind of a shame that this thing that represents a religion of justice and compassion, which is what it means to Jews, to a lot of people in the world that are impacted by that conflict it's an image of what was oppression for them.

Despite the shift in her view of Jews, Safia still sees one major difference between the two groups which she believes helps perpetuate the conflict. When asked what she thinks would be the optimal way to end the conflict, she said:

> The best solution would be one state for everybody where everybody is equal. Everybody living there is an equal citizen, like in America, which will probably never happen because even kind, compassionate Jews, as much as they believe in the American way of democracy, they feel like when it comes to Israel it's a different story. It has to be just this little Jewish majority state. It has to be a Jewish place because that's the only way it can be safe, if it's Jewish. So ideally it would be one state—that's what the ethical, moral thing is. But at least two states that one has a chance of being

> a real state, not just little ghettos of Swiss cheese of pieces of land.

Mansur sees the second generation as relating to the conflict differently than the first because of their upbringing in a more stable and predictable society. He spoke about his family's hardships in traveling back to and within Palestine:

> I personally did not mind, but the kids, like every time I'd take them they were searched. They get used to the freedom and the luxury of the United States and it is sort of difficult. So now we go every three years, four years. It's really not as frequent as it used to be before.

Gameel has acquired a more optimistic outlook on the future of the conflict based on the experiences of the second generation who have grown up in democratic America. Since they have not endured their parents' statelessness, he views them as better equipped to actualize change in the Israeli-occupied territories:

> I think that in the second generation there's more hope for them to make a change because they're not afraid like their parents might have been, because they've grown up as Americans and they know that they have rights . . . that they are capable of making change, of using their politicians to effect that change and to talk about the situation. So I think that, yes, they're much more empowered and are continuing to become more empowered.

SECOND GENERATION PALESTINIAN AMERICANS

Gameel's perspective on the second generation does not hold true for its members who grew up exiled in the Middle East. Their background experience with conflict and displacement demarcates them from other members of the second generation who grew up in the States instead of refugee camps (Ben-Ze'ev, 2005). Burhan knows what it is like to be stateless. Because of his experiences as a refugee in Kuwait, where he was looked down upon and given no rights, he has come to despise the idea of national borders. Asim told a very similar story. He also came to the United States from Kuwait with refugee status. After all of his struggles, he has concluded that instead of claiming a national identity, it is easier to "be a Muslim and not really mess with this thing, because this is what politics does; it creates confusion and prejudices." This outlook is common among the post-WWII generation, who tend towards a pan-Arab identity, often rooted in Islam (Wald, 2009).

When he was a young adult, Burhan secured a visa to attend college in North Carolina. He remembers walking the streets of downtown Raleigh, noting the cultural norms of Americans:

> I would look through the storefronts to see how people eat. Do they eat like me? I've always had an impression of Americans being completely different than us. And I've always been, since I was a little kid, the entire world is a playground for me… I never believed and recognized borders. I've always felt that they were made by men, manned by men to control man… So I was here and that experience… when I came here by the way, I couldn't go back to Kuwait anymore. That's that. Nobody will take me and the United States could actually pick me up and deport me and they don't know where to go with me. There's no other country would accept me.

Becoming an American citizen was a turning point for Burhan, as it marked the first time he could freely travel the globe:

> When I first got my American passport you could've offered me a billion dollars or the passport and I would've taken the passport. I never felt free in my life until that day because I can put that passport in my pocket and travel and go anywhere. And I did!

As well as serving as a board member of the Arab American Anti-Discrimination Committee and being affiliated with the American Arab Institute, Ahmed was president of a local Palestinian organization. As Hassan mentioned before, participation in local groups declined after 9/11, and this particular organization had been more or less inactive for three years. The group was originally created to help local Palestinians retain a sense of their community and culture, especially those Americanized children who otherwise might not even learn to speak Arabic. This club and a local Islamic center, with its associated school (to which several respondents, including Yasir, send their children), appear to serve as cultural institutions reinforcing the community, its ethnic practices, and its identities, much as the synagogue and Jewish youth groups do for Israeli American subjects and their children (Gold, 2007; Rebhun & Lev Ari, 2010).

Most of the younger Palestinians are involved in on-campus groups related to their ethnicity or the conflict, such as the Muslim Student Association and the Middle Eastern North African Student Association. Naimah takes Arabic classes to improve her communication skills while in Arab nations and with her extended family (her parents still live in Kuwait). Hana noted that "…every [campus] event that I see about the conflict or that's Palestinian related, I try to attend." Adara spoke about the strong associations between the Jewish student group, Hillel, and the Arab or Muslim groups at her university, and how they create dialogues and events in support of a peaceful resolution to the conflict. Raya told me that she is so heavily involved in her college's Hillel, "I'm pretty much the honorary Jew."

Adara differentiates between Jewish Americans who support Palestinian rights and "…somebody who is a Zionist, for example, who's just so strong in Israel's right to exist that they just want to wipe out the Palestinians. There's no way you can see eye-to-eye with somebody like that." Naimah also has trouble understanding and dealing with people who think this way: "I meet some Jewish people and they totally support Zionism, and I think, how can you support it on a… you know, human rights level?" When asked for an example of the latter kind of Jewish American, Adara provided the following case:

> I have a Palestine necklace that's in the shape of the country and it's got the flag on it. I wear that a lot. And one guy saw it and he's like, "Oh so you're Israeli?" I was like, "No, I am actually Palestinian." He's like, "There's no such thing as Palestine," and he tried to get into an argument with me. He was Israeli and this was at work actually. My manager was like, just let it go, don't deal with it. People are just very adamant when they find out you're Palestinian. They just want to prove you wrong and get you all riled up for no reason.

Hana has encountered similar types of prejudice:

> For me it's tough because it's like, I am a Palestinian American, but then I feel like not as many people really... they may have heard of Palestine but they don't recognize it... People don't always recognize it as an actual country. They just think of the conflict and they don't think of the positives of this group of people. And I just feel like there's no recognition.

Adara is additionally distressed by the United States at the institutional level, and believes that American foreign policy in general is misguided. The overall impression that the second generation has regarding America's role in the conflict is well-articulated by Adara:

> I think it needs to be looked at and revised. I think it's very biased against the Palestinian people. The U. S. government supports the Israeli government. They give them money. A lot of the tax money goes to the Israeli government, to the IDF, which is the Israeli Defense Force. It goes straight to them, the weapons that they're using to kill all these Palestinians and to destroy their homes is funded by the American government. So it's definitely an issue for me.

These thoughts reflect those previously expressed by first generation Palestinians. The group's main conviction was summed up by Yasir: "It's in the national interest of this country to support Israel... This is my land and I care about it a lot, and it hurts me that the government are one-sided." As to why they think the U.S. unequivocally supports Israel, these subjects mentioned a range of possibilities, from the influence of the Jewish lobby, to economic interests (such as access to oil) in the Middle East, to speculations about Christian fundamentalism and the prophesized Rapture.[2]

---

[2] The Rapture refers to the Christian belief that Jesus will one day return to earth and save his followers from the oncoming apocalypse, which will destroy the rest of mankind. This Second Coming of Jesus, according to some fundamentalist interpretations of the Book of Revelation, will only happen if the State of Israel is in existence. A succinct discussion of this belief can be

Much like the others, Asim and Josef feel conflicted about living in a land that does nothing to stop the affliction of their people. Asim avowed, "I feel like honestly, honestly, truly, the U.S. politics do have a lot to do with the conflict. The U.S. politics could have a very good role in ending this conflict." Josef elaborated:

> ...There is a sense that if the U.S. really wanted things to be different there, then they could exert enough pressure that things could be different there. I mean, with the billions of dollars of aid that we send over there and the military support, you know if things really wanted to be different they could issue enough leverage to make it different. So there's a sense that they don't want things to be a whole lot different.

Josef thinks Americans are given a misleading image of Palestinians and Israelis. He maintains that knowing the actual history of the land is an important step in promoting a fair resolution. Josef referred to early Zionist activist groups, such as Irgun, and events such as the Deir Yassin massacre,[3] to support his argument that Jews were the ones

> who initially imported terrorism into the Middle East... And so there's a history that a fair number of people have, most of the U.S. does not have, that recognizes that this is not a group of barbaric, hedonistic, terroristic Palestinians fighting these poor Israelis who are just trying to have a place to live.

---

found in Deborah Caldwell's "The rapture factor: Why conservative Christians' love of Israel is intertwined with the Battle of Armageddon."

[3] Irgun was a militant Zionist group operating in Palestine between 1931 and 1948. Their attacks were mainly aimed at British authorities and Palestinian inhabitants, as they fought for Jewish rights to the Holy Land. The Deir Yassin massacre was an event carried out by Irgun and others on the village of Deir Yassin, which had declared its neutrality during the 1948 Arab-Israeli War. Between 110 and 140 Arab villagers, including women, children and the elderly, were killed (Hogan, 2001). A Jewish settlement was built partially over the village site. For more information, please refer to Matthew Hogan's 2001 article "The 1948 Massacre at Deir Yassin Revisited" and Noam Chomsky's 1999 book, *Fateful Triangle: The United States, Israel and the Palestinians.*

Such accounts contest the more recognized colonization narratives and their "active disremembering" (Ram, 2009), thus giving Palestinians greater agency regarding their future (Lentin, 2009). By referring to nakba stories, Palestinians such as Josef use collective memories to fortify their national identity; the stories also serve as active forms of resistance (Lentin, 2009).

Facing Palestinian stereotypes such as those he describes above has shaped Josef over time, making him more "willing to speak out about things." He has transformed from being "embarrassed to being proud, to being primarily just angry and feeling futile, to a sense that things could change and things can change."

Ahmed made an important point about the shifting image of the U.S. in the Middle East and how this change bears upon him as someone who feels connected to both his Palestinian and American identities:

> I hate the connection that I have to America whenever I go overseas. And especially with the War in Iraq it makes it even worse. People overseas cannot understand why is America teddy-bearing Israel so bad, to the point that people have all kinds of theories about Israelis running the U.S… You know, when I first came here I used to go [back home] every year once or twice, and my nephews and nieces were like, "Oh Uncle, how is America? So beautiful, we want to go there." And in the past few years they look at me and say, "We just cannot understand why you would live in such a hateful country."

Asim touched on more general themes of belonging, ethnicity, and identity when asked how he identifies himself:

> …I'm a U.S. citizen, yes. Because you know, as soon as you say U.S. citizen they say, yeah I know that, where are you really from? Usually it's more appropriate to say where you are originally from than to say U.S. citizen. That's the challenge we go through as foreign Americans, particularly as Palestinians.

His reflections speak to the meaningful differences between self-ascribed identities and those which are imposed by others, showing how both types matter for how we view ourselves and our social location.

Yasir, Asim, and Adara all mentioned personal encounters with discrimination in America. Their feelings and experiences proved typical among Palestinian subjects. Especially since the events of 9/11, there has been a dramatic increase in individual-level acts of discrimination (Gold & Bozorgmehr, 2007; Portes & Rumbaut, 2006). Yasir spoke about living as a Palestinian in post-September 11th America:

> Our wives were harassed in the shopping centers and malls… the wives more than us because they are marked [by wearing traditional Muslim veils]. You know, they get flipped the finger, and for us you get comments, "Why don't you go back home?"

Asim added the following:

> You know like when black people say you don't know what it's like to have gone through slavery or walk around as a black person? I remember that right after 9/11, I suddenly had a feeling that now I see what black people… like everywhere you are, you understand. Like at the airport, they'll be in your luggage and everyone is looking at you differently. That feeling sucks. All the sudden everybody looks at you and you are afraid.

Adara has come across people who ascribe to the media-driven stereotype equating "Palestinian" with "terrorist," but she has also come across many Americans who recognize that these stereotypes cannot and should not be applied at the individual level:

> *Adara*: Well, dealing with people stateside, a lot of people just have the mentality that all Palestinians are terrorists. So when I say I'm Palestinian to somebody, it kind of takes them by shock because they're like, well, you're not a terrorist. So it's just hard to identify with it because people always have this preset mentality of what they think you are, and then when

> they meet you and they see that you're nothing like what they think, it's just hard to deal with that.
>
> *Interviewer*: So how do you think that affects your identity? Does it make you think of your Palestinian identity more?
>
> *Adara*: Definitely. It makes me even prouder to be who I am and to just break all these stereotypes left and right. Because there were so many people after September 11th who came up to me and were like, we know that whoever's responsible, we know that all Muslims or all Arabs are not like this, because they knew who I was. So it makes me a stronger person and it makes me so much more proud of who I am and my heritage.

Hana discussed her similar experiences:

> *Hana*: …If I'm talking to somebody online, like on a message board, and I mention that I'm Palestinian American, then it's like, "Oh my God, terrorist, terrorist," you know? It's jokingly, but still, for me it's like, you have no idea. You know, you're completely clueless and you shouldn't just assume these things or say it at all…
>
> *Interviewer*: When people say stuff like that, how does it affect your connection to the conflict?
>
> *Hana*: It sort of strengthens me with other Arabs and Palestinians, and maybe with more of the cliché American stereotype type people, I sort of isolate myself from them… but then I also want to educate them too. So I think it overall strengthens me because it makes me voice my opinions and my thoughts and my knowledge more than it used to.

Hana and Adara's stories bring us back to the discussion with Israeli subjects about how they would feel in a hypothetical situation where America is pro-Palestinian. Dalia and Leah both said they would feel more of an urge to act on behalf of Israel in this case, in order to help garner support for their people, and thought that facing discrimination would actually strengthen their ethnic identity as they worked to dismantle stereotypes. In Adara and Hana's statements, we hear real-world echoes of the Jewish Israeli Americans' imagined reactions.

Ahmed cited an unusual encounter with a Jewish American at an international festival in Raleigh five years earlier:

> I was sitting at the Palestinian booth and of course with my Palestinian outfit on. And a lady comes by and she was like, "Hi, how are you?" And she was very anxious to talk to someone. And I was talking to her and she was like, "You know what?" She was like, "I'm Jewish." I was like, "It's alright, I'm Muslim, you're Jewish." And she's like, "No, I want to tell you. I went to Israel/Palestine last year, and my husband and I were very pro-Israeli. We just hated anything called Palestinian." And I was like, "Okay, I might be the wrong person to tell that to, but okay." [He laughs.] And then she was like, "But we stayed there. One month later we moved from Tel Aviv to Ramallah and we became pro-Palestinian, anti-Israeli." And I was like, "Whoa, what happened?" She was like, "We witnessed, on the ground, what was happening, what was going on . . . we did not have to do more than reading the *Maariv* and *Yedioth Ahronoth* [Israeli newspapers] , and these things opened our minds…" So here's a woman that of course has nothing to do with the conflict, I would say, and she still was very Zionist. And she went there and converted 180 degrees. That's how people educated people about the truth… and that's how the conflict does affect people's mentality.

This encounter taught Ahmed that not all Jewish Americans unquestioningly support Israel. It also works to reinforce the notion that direct experiences with conflict have a discernable, transformative impact on identity—in some cases, such as this one, an impact that reshapes preexisting notions of identity. Burhan had an interaction similar to Ahmed's international festival incident:

> I was talking to an Israeli journalist at one of the universities here. He came and introduced himself after I gave a lecture to a group of students. He is an Israeli, he grew up in a kibbutz. And his impression of Palestinians is that they need to be killed, eliminated, wiped out. Nobody should survive, or [they should be] driven off the land. He went to Tel Aviv to the university to study journalism. And he said, "I started reading

> from Edward Said." And he said, "I was so angry at all the lies I was told about the Palestinians." He was so mad that recently he was involved in a play where he portrayed himself as a Palestinian, and the Palestinian portrayed himself as an Israeli soldier.

Hana also claims she has in fact often been well-received as a Palestinian American. She thinks such positive interactions are linked to her generational status:

> …I haven't met any Jewish people that when they find out I am Palestinian have any anger. And I think it's because our generation has been raised to sort of look at everything in an open-minded way. Looking at it as if what's happening right now, this was our fathers' generation that has so much anger and rage and fighting.

Like Hana, Raya believes generational differences affect her sense of belonging in America and her Palestinian identity. When asked if she has ever considered moving to Palestine, she told me:

> I think that I belong in America because, and I always debate with my parents about this, but I think that if I go over there, no matter what, they're going to think that I'm not one of them. No one will ever accept me… because I'm American, because I am different. Even the way I speak. And I really think, I feel like I belong in America because this is my culture, to a certain extent, and I feel accepted here. What's unique about America is that… if you're born in America, you're American.

Yasir, like the others, has not suffered much discrimination in the United States; however, he is concerned about American attitudes towards Arabs and Muslims, especially considering current relations with Iraq and other Islamic nations. His fears are reminiscent of Israeli American subjects' anxieties about a possible future recurrence of anti-Semitism and the end of America's support for Israel:

> You know, to tell you the truth, I am American now, but I'm not comfortable 100%. What happened in the past, with the Japanese in the concentration camps, at any minute another Bin Laden will arise from somewhere and do something stupid. And who pays for it? Everybody who looks like me, everybody who looks like my wife with the veil, my kids… Although we've been living here, paying taxes, been in this country, all of our kids, that's all they know this country, we have businesses… This is not going to help us by an ignorant… I mean we've had very little of it, but I'm afraid the next one is going to be a total mess… The first time, in 2001, we had very few comments, very few people bothered us, and a lot of people called and asked to help us—Americans. They offered their sympathy, their help… neighbors, parents on the kids' soccer teams, business associates, stuff like that, and they were nice. I'm afraid half of these people will change their mind if anything happens again.

Burhan noted how in today's world we are simply not as isolated from one another as we would sometimes like to believe. Like many other respondents from both ethnic groups, Burhan thinks that if people were willing to take more active roles in understanding and alleviating the suffering of others—as opposed to viewing them as foreign, distant Others, or to merely claiming sympathy—then global ethnic conflicts might be closer to resolution:

> Israelis are not suffering like the Palestinians. The vast majority… maybe the ones that are close to the West Bank or some of the settlements, but… proper Israel truly don't know what's going on in Gaza and the West Bank. They don't see the suffering. It is just like us here in the United States. Most Americans truly might sympathize with something, a cause or another, but because it's not directly impacting our lives and our security and our safety, we don't do anything. We sympathize. We sympathize with the Iraqis. We sympathized with the Rwandans when they got massacred—one million of them got killed—but that's all we do, because it doesn't impact me sitting here having a great cup of coffee talking to you. It doesn't impact me buying things and going on

> vacations. It doesn't take anything away from me. And that is so selfish. If that is the only way you can feel the pain of other people… the pain is going to come to us because it is going to spread.

In alignment with canons of conflict theory, Burhan believes that the solution to the conflict in Israel/Palestine lies largely in increased interaction and interdependence. Inter-cultural conflict can be so resistant to resolution because perceived threat causes individuals to avoid interactions with the Other and shun those that do (Worchel, 2005):

> There are different groups right now because there's boundaries that have been put up to separate the people. And as you separate people from each other they become more… when you have very little contact with a group of people, you don't trust them. Let me give you a scenario. Imagine there is a Palestinian state and there's Israel, open borders… What happens is commerce, money. Money solves and erases a lot of history. Common interests will make you friends. Why? Because that is the human nature of things.

CONCLUSIONS

Jewish Israeli Americans are cognizant and appreciative of the power of the Jewish lobby and America's pro-Israel stance regarding the conflict. They recognize these two elements as enormously important for Israel's strength and survival. Such positive experiences with reception make it easier for these transnationals to maintain homeland ties and hybridized identities while successfully integrating into their host country. This receptivity also contributes to second generation Jewish Israelis' selective acculturation. It facilitates a smooth process of preserving important aspects of their parents' heritage while largely assimilating into mainstream American culture and forming American identities.

Palestinian Americans face an unusual predicament as they confront their oppositional feelings towards the host country. On the one hand, they are incredibly grateful for finally having a place to belong and for being granted civil rights and citizenship—a cherished status previously denied to them by Israel as well as surrounding Arab nations that took them in as refugees. Despite this gratitude towards America, they cannot escape the guilt that comes with feeling that their hard-earned new freedoms literally come with a price they must pay, in the form of taxes that go toward funding the Israeli occupation of Palestine. Such feelings reverberate across the generations, from those who retain memories of the conflict, to those who remember hardships experienced as refugees in the Middle East, and those who never endured the conflict but have been socialized within a culture fundamentally transformed by it.

Conclusion

In assessing the claims and contributions of this book, I find it useful to begin by restating the central aims of my study. First and foremost, I wanted to examine the relationship between transnational identity and conflict, and, more specifically, whether or not diasporic identity is affected by homeland conflict. This initial query stemmed from my response to Tilly's (2002) claim that identity is primarily influenced by conflict at the actual site, and that away from the center of the conflict it tends to dissipate. Having studied in Israel and having known several Jewish Israeli and Palestinian Americans throughout my life, I questioned whether or not this assertion always held true, as the people I had encountered were constantly discussing and reflecting on the ongoing Israeli-Palestinian conflict. It was clear to me that this conflict continued to be an integral part of their lives in the United States, and it seemed that it played a significant role in how they see themselves as Jewish Israeli or Palestinian Americans. Through the words of Palestinian and Jewish Israeli Americans interviewees, I have demonstrated throughout this book how homeland conflict, whether personally or vicariously experienced, does have a long-lasting impact on these individuals and their diasporic identities. In my examination of differences by generational status and ethnic group, I have come to several conclusions.

Generational differences are notable in the degree to which the conflict in Israel/Palestine influences subjects' current lives in the diaspora. In support of transnationalism and immigration scholarship (Haller and Landolt, 2005; Levitt, 2009; Levitt & Jaworsky, 2007;

Levitt & Waters, 2002; Portes et al., 2009; Portes and Rumbaut, 2005; Waters et al., 2010; Zhou, 1997) which concluded that the first generation are much more likely to orient their lives around homeland events, I discovered that first generation Jewish Israeli and Palestinian Americans maintain a stronger connection to conflict and the homeland than their children. Second generation individuals from both ethnic groups were not primarily raised in the country of origin and lack their parents' immigrant and/or refugee pasts. While the first generation was socialized within a culture consistently focused on the Israeli-Palestinian struggle and retains vivid and often terrifying memories of the conflict, for the most part (with the exception of Palestinians raised in refugee camps), those of the second generation only know their lives in the U.S. Secondly, the first generation continues to maintain more significant connections to the conflict, in many cases because of fear for the safety of members of their nuclear family unit who are still living in the homeland.

Retention and reiteration of parents' shared memories and firsthand stories about strife experienced in Israel/Palestine was discovered to be a central mechanism linking both the first and second generation to the homeland and its ongoing conflict. Accounts are powerful in shaping the way people view themselves and their social world, and, through the narratives, memories, and discourses they hear, Jewish Israeli and Palestinian American children have been socialized to remain continually invested in the conflict.

For Jewish Israelis, collective memories related to the conflict emphasize the necessity of Israel's continued existence, "just in case." For them, the Israeli-Palestinian conflict is the latest phase in a long-standing history of Jewish oppression. For Palestinians, collective memories about their ancestors living in villages in Palestine and owning deeds to the land are major factors that keep them longing for home and waiting for a right to return from within their transnational lives. They too remember the history of the Holocaust and the subsequent founding of Israel, but for them, this memory is one in which Jews shifted roles, from the persecuted to the persecutors. Meanwhile, for Jewish Israelis the same narrative is about arriving in a safe haven after an encounter with the most monstrous kind of evil.

In their personal memories of experience with homeland conflict, there are also key differences by ethnic group—in conceptualizations of conflict and in frequency of occurrence. Jewish Israeli Americans cited events such as suicide bombings, Intifadas, and military service when describing their own history with the conflict. They also frequently mentioned how conflict in Israel was just one aspect of their lives and did not consume their entire existence there. Nevertheless, the fears and anxieties accumulated in their experiences with conflict follow them into the diaspora, where they act to continually focus immigrants' attention on homeland happenings. Palestinian Americans also preserve their ties to the conflict-ridden homeland through shared personal accounts, but in their stories, conflict pervaded nearly every aspect of homeland existence, from their daily routines—which were encumbered by military checkpoints and ever-shifting blockades—to their lack of citizenship rights. First generation Palestinian Americans lived in communities, described by some as virtual prisons, where they were often denied basic civil liberties. Many were evicted from their homes and became destitute refugees. These experiences are not easily forgotten despite the Palestinians' relocation to the other side of the world, and by continually sharing their memories of displacement with their children, these immigrants reinforce the importance of the conflict and the homeland in both generations' diasporic lives.

The second core area of this study, as discussed in Chapter Three, involves ethnic and generational differences in accessing information about homeland conflict. I observed that subjects predominantly rely on two major types of resources—mass media, and personal connections to individuals still living within the homeland. The first generation, with their more extensive homeland social networks, depend more often on people in Israel/Palestine to acquire information than do their less-connected children; they also used more homeland-based and international media sources. This is due, in part, to their comfort and familiarity with Middle Eastern reporting. In contrast, their Americanized children usually watch mainstream U.S. sources or rely on their parents for information about homeland conflict. And as I had anticipated, the first generation more frequently access and are more emotionally impacted by reports on the conflict than the second generation.

As for contrasts by ethnic group in this area, Palestinian Americans appear to be somewhat more aware of and burdened by the conflict than Jewish Israeli Americans, as it remains a daily issue of great concern for their people back home. This is in contrast to the more intermittent experiences with hardship and violence that most Jewish Israelis reported. As mentioned earlier, all but one of the first generation Palestinian Americans said that they are "informed daily" and are "totally informed," while only three Jewish Israelis of the first generation get news on a daily basis and only one felt "totally informed." The level of perceived personal knowledge about the current state of the conflict was much higher for members of both Palestinian American generations.

Both groups consistently report hostile-media perceptions. Purposely seeking out "hostile" media is a prevalent trend among Palestinian respondents, but this trend is noticeably absent among the Jewish Israelis. In speculating on why Palestinians actively consume media they perceive as pro-Israeli, it may be worth noting the significance of America's role in the conflict and of American media coverage of the strife, both of which are seen by Palestinians as lending greater support to the Israeli side. It makes sense that these individuals would try to "keep their ears to the ground" and remain aware of the dominant discourse in their host country as they navigate their immigrant status and lives—especially when that dominant discourse is perceived as intertwined with the suffering of fellow group members in the homeland.

The presence of certain observed differences by ethnic group notwithstanding, it is important to come back to the overall significant diasporic identity effects found to result from conflict. The most important conclusion drawn from this third chapter is congruent with that of the second—almost all members of these two ethnic groups make some kind of effort to remain informed about current conflict in the homeland, and they all feel influenced by the state of the conflict (and the state of its media coverage) despite their physical distance from it. Once again, it is clear that perceptions of homeland conflict are significant for identity formation and maintenance processes.

When it comes to their lives in the United States, Palestinians unanimously describe distress over living in a nation that partially funds the opposing side of the conflict, while also noting their great love and appreciation for their new country, with its guaranteed freedoms and personal rights (which many of them have never before received, either in Palestine or elsewhere in the Middle East). Palestinians come to America shouldering many lingering effects of homeland conflict. They face difficulties with national recognition, with representation in the media, and with rights and capabilities to return to or even visit the homeland (Bishara, 2008; Hanafi, 2005; Marvasti & McKinney, 2004; Matar, 2006; Noakes & Wilkins, 2002).

Members of the second generation often also know the effects of dispossession and discrimination, since many spent their youths in the Middle East as refugees (Ben Ze-ev, 2005). In contrast, Jewish emigrants from Israel are for the most part highly successful, voluntary immigrants who left in search of better economic and educational opportunities in the United States—a nation they view as supportive of their homeland (Gold, 1997, 2002, 2007; Rebhun and Lev Ari, 2010). Jewish Israelis are grateful for the historical and continuing assistance provided to Israel by the United States, and believe it is necessary to secure the future existence of Israel as an independent nation. Nevertheless, Israeli immigrants do tend to continually see themselves as Israeli first and foremost, and most retain plans to return, something they often do (Gold, 1997, 2002, 2007; Rebhun & Lev Ari, 2010).

It has been claimed by many scholars of American and Middle East relations that Palestinians have experienced less acceptance in the United States than Jews and Jewish Israelis (Ackerman, 2001; Barghouti, 1988; Chomsky, 2010; Dunsky, 2008; Ellis, 2009; Khalidi, 1997; Said, 1979; Shain, 1996). And indeed, Palestinian respondents describe how mass media portrayals and government actions, especially after the events of September 11th, have negatively impacted their reception and treatment by Americans. They also claim that this prejudice has made it more difficult for Palestinians to advocate on behalf of their homeland. Palestinian transnational movements in the U.S. are notably weaker and less visible as compared to the relatively powerful Jewish and Israeli lobby in the United States (Bishara, 2008; Wald, 2009). I discovered that for both populations, perceptions of American receptivity work to strengthen their diasporic identities. For Jewish Israelis, their mostly positive experiences in the U.S. enable the process of selective acculturation. They are able to preserve homeland connections through participating in Jewish communities and transnational organizations, while they simultaneously assimilate successfully into American society. Palestinian American immigrants who face stigmatization and perceived unequal treatment in America see these experiences as part of a pattern of injustices committed against their people; this leads them to further identify themselves with their ancestry and the homeland. And yet Palestinian Americans also report many positive encounters in the U.S., ranging from shows of community support after 9/11, to productive conflict-related discussions with acquaintances, to inter-group activist work, and even to tales of "conversion narratives" shared with them by former Zionists. For both groups, their American diaspora experiences, negative and positive, work to fortify their ethnic identity and connections to homeland conflict despite their out-migration.

This study presents new ways of understanding and examining transnational identity in relation to homeland conflict. My approach fits well, I believe, in an increasingly interconnected world where transnationalism has initiated new ways of comprehending identity and its multiplicities. Work on the impact of globalization and on transnational communities is the inevitable future of ethnic identity studies, and my analysis here contributes to this burgeoning literature. Besides adding to studies of ethnic and diasporic identities, my work also promotes the value of qualitative methodologies. By using personal narratives, accounts, and social memories to inductively explore how individuals do identity and boundary work, I allow for subjects to explain in their own words, often at length, the intricate processes involved. I argue that the use of in-depth, open-ended interviewing techniques is an important step towards attempting to balance out power differentials between researcher and respondent, towards gaining a deeper, more realistic understanding of identity, and towards progress in the social sciences.

Despite the important contributions of this study, some key limitations should be addressed. The very fact that I emphasized conflict as a subject and frame in the interviews created the possibility that the topic would be overrepresented in responses. I attempted to work against this danger by informing potential interviewees only that I was interested in exploring how immigrants in the diaspora relate to the homeland. When we met for the face-to-face interviews, I began by gathering basic demographic information and then asked each respondent to list homeland issues that were important to him or her as an Israeli or Palestinian living in the U.S.[1] I only asked about conflict if it had not already been mentioned, which, as it turned out, was the case with just one respondent. Nevertheless, since the interview guide was centered on exploring the connections between homeland conflict and identity, this limitation remains pertinent.

Regarding my choice to use stories and memories as a means of examining how conflict affects identity in the diaspora, it is important to note that collective memories and shared stories from the past

---

[1] Please refer to Appendix A.

typically should not be empirically used to gather historical facts. Instead, they should be treated as reconstructions of the past used by individuals to make sense of their current lives, often for persuasive purposes for themselves and others (Fivush, 2008; Halbwachs, 1992; Huttunen, 2005; Keightley, 2010; Lentin, 2009; Misztal, 2010; Nets-Zehngut, 2008; Olick, 1999; Orbuch, 1997; Ram, 2009; Schwartz, 1996; Yerushalmi, 1982). Stories' rhetorical and identity-building effects are primary reasons why so many have chosen memory and narrative methodologies to explore the social construction of transnational identities (Chamberlain & Leydesdorff, 2004; Eastmond, 2007; El-Aswad, 2006; Hammer, 2005; Langfield, 2009; Misztal, 2010; Ram, 2009; Trew, 2010). I believe that I heard many powerful truths from my respondents, but I am aware that my methods have the potential to solicit data that are misremembered, ill-informed, or distorted—sometimes, perhaps, intentionally so.

The range of background variables for my sample was also limited, although in a community study this is a mostly unavoidable issue, and I made great efforts to locate a sample of individuals diverse in many aspects. I found it difficult to locate first generation Palestinian American women who were willing to speak with me, and so there is unequal gender representation within this group of respondents. The overall distribution ratio of males to females was also unbalanced. It would be interesting and worthwhile to explore why women among this group were less keen to be interviewed, especially since I did not describe the study to respondents as being about conflict per se. I also maintain that gender is an important variable in need of greater exploration in its relation to homeland conflict and identity. Recent studies looking at Jewish Israeli women's diasporic identity have found that although women are commonly allotted the important responsibility of creating a nurturing home environment that reflects and reinforces homeland values and practices (Gans, 2007; Georgiou, 2006; Gold, 2007), their voices are largely silenced within public discussions of Israel and the conflict with Palestinians (Georgiou, 2006; Sztokman, 2007). This fact may have important consequences, considering that women are commonly found to challenge binary notions of "us and them" in relation to conflict (Sztokman, 2007). Future studies should further examine the important perspectives and contributions of women regarding homeland conflict, and why and how they seem to be consistently suppressed.

Additionally, although this study's sample included a broad range of occupations and incomes, there was certainly a preponderance of highly-educated and mostly middle- to upper-class people. This was partly because of the high percentage of well-educated individuals living in the Research Triangle area, and also likely because of the higher average level of education and occupational expertise among Jewish Israelis (Gold, 2007; Rebhun & Lev Ari, 2010) and Middle Easterners overall (Gold & Bozorgmehr, 2007) in the United States. The sampling variance may also have been impacted by personal characteristics of those I was able to connect with through social networking, and of those willing to be interviewed by me. Given the attitudes reflected in many of the responses I received, I think it is possible that individuals with more progressive perspectives regarding the conflict may have been the most interested and willing to talk with me. Lastly, since the average age of the first generation respondents was in the 40s, it is certainly possible that results would have been different had I been able to speak with older individuals, especially given the significance of early-twentieth-century events in the Israeli-Palestinian conflict.

There is, furthermore, always the chance that subjects will alter and circumscribe their responses based on their perceptions of what the researcher is seeking and what the researcher represents for the respondent. I have previously discussed some of the ways that my own status as a Jewish American may have swayed subjects' responses. For example, I more often heard Jewish Israeli subjects express extreme negative feelings about Palestinians than vice versa, and Jewish Israelis were more vocal in their support of "any means necessary" tactics against the other side. Indeed, I never heard Palestinian Americans express some of the perspectives attributed to them in popular discourse, such as beliefs that Israel should be obliterated. While it is certainly true that interviewees (on both sides) may have curbed their responses for fear of offending me or having their views published, I worked hard to ensure all respondents that my goal was to listen and not to judge, and that their identities would be protected. I believe that, overall, respondents shared their stories and their views with remarkable frankness. I attempted to use subjects' own words as often as possible to minimize the dangers of inaccurately representing them, and I actively sought to use outlying responses throughout my analyses as a way to work against overgeneralization.

It is my sincere hope that this study will provide useful material and suggest productive future research directions for other scholars of global conflicts and transnational identity. And perhaps it will contribute, in some tiny way, to conditions facilitating eventual resolution of the Israeli-Palestinian conflict.

Appendix A: Interview Guide

Demographics:

What is your current age?

Are you married or single? Have you been married before? How many times?

Do you have any children or dependents? If not, do you plan on having children?

What languages do you speak?

What is the highest level of education that you have completed?

Are you an American citizen? Are you a permanent resident? Do you have a visa?

What do you identify yourself as—ethnically or racially?

Do you practice a religion? If yes, what denomination are you? Did your family practice a religion when you were growing up? (*If married*) Does your spouse practice any religion? (*If they have kids*) Do your kids?

Where were you born? (*Family background*)

How long have you lived in the United States?

If not for your entire life, name all of the places where you have lived prior to living in the United States?

Do you see Israel/Palestine as your homeland?

How often, if ever, do you visit there?

Do you think that you will eventually return to Israel/Palestine?

Question #1: What are some homeland issues that are important to you as a Palestinian/Jewish Israeli living in the United States? How would you rank them in order of importance to you as a Palestinian/Israeli American? (*If conflict is not mentioned*) Is homeland conflict something you think about a lot as a Palestinian/Jewish Israeli in the United States? Where would that fall in your ranking?

Question #2: Since living in America, please describe for me a homeland event that you consider to be an instance of conflict. What types of activity would fit with your concept of conflict in Israel/Palestine? (*If they still do not have an answer*) Which type of homeland event best fits with your concept of conflict—A) Military occupation of land and homes, B) denial of civil liberties, C) military-related violence, or D) a bus bombing?

Question #3: Now describe for me your reactions and feelings surrounding such an occurrence of conflict. Would you say that these feelings represent your typical reaction to homeland conflict? If not, how would you describe your usual reaction to conflict in general?

Question #4: What is it about this specific type of conflict that makes it significant to you even though you no longer live there?

Question #5: In what ways, if any, do you think that conflict in Israel/Palestine affects the way you think of yourself?

Question #6: Does the conflict make any of the boundaries/divides between different groups stronger for you? To give you some potential examples—Jewish versus Israeli, Palestinian versus Arab, Palestinian versus Jewish Israeli, Palestinian/Jewish Israeli versus Palestinian/Jewish Israeli American, Palestinian American versus Jewish Israeli American.

Question #7: In regards to the group divide, please describe some of the significant differences between you and someone in the other group.

Question #8: Can you come up with any ways that you think an instance of conflict would have a different impact on you as compared to someone in the other group?

Question #9: Do you think there is any connection between your opinions and reactions to homeland conflict and the history of your people?

Question #10: Do you think that your attitudes and feelings about homeland conflict are different now than in the past, based on your current lifestyle and stage in life?

Question #11: Please list for me your membership in any organizations related to being a Palestinian/Israeli/Jew/Arab/Palestinian American/Jewish Israeli American. (*If they cannot think of any*) A few examples of organizations are: religious institutions or groups—like a synagogue/mosque or prayer group, organizations supporting relations between America and Palestine/Israel, programs aimed at developing peace between Palestinians and Jews, and college campus groups. On average, how often would you say you are typically actively involved in these organizations—every day, every week or so, every month or so, a few times a year, or once a year or less?

Question #12: Please describe for me your personal connections (such as family members or friends) with people linked to Palestine or Israel, both here in America and there. On average, how often would you say you are typically in contact with them? Can you estimate how many of these people know each other? If you had to make your best guess, what percentage of your personal connections here in the U.S. are to other people linked to Israel/Palestine?

Question #13: How do you receive information about conflict in Palestine/Israel? Which source do you think you most often rely upon, and how much of the time?

Question #14: On average, which of the following best represents how *often* you are informed about homeland conflict—every day, every week or so, every month or so, a few times a year, or never? As far as keeping up to date on homeland conflict, do you feel that you are most often uninformed, somewhat informed, mostly informed, or totally informed?

Question #15: For the next two questions, I am asking you to compare yourself to someone (*for first generation*) whose parents lived in Israel/Palestine but they're American-born **or** (*for second generation*) who lived in Israel/Palestine. Do you think that there are differences between you and someone in the other category in how you access information about homeland conflict? Do you think that there are differences in how you react to information about homeland conflict? And now, comparing yourself to someone like a Jewish/Arab American, someone who is still connected but less directly, do you think there are any differences in these same two areas?

Question #16: (*For first generation immigrants*) If there were any, please describe for me a few experiences you had while living in Palestine/Israel that continue to influence your connection to the conflict there today. (*For second generation immigrants only*) Do you think that your attitudes and feelings about homeland conflict were changed by any specific events?

Question #17: Now please describe for me any interactions you've had during your childhood or adulthood with people here in America that you feel have either strengthened or weakened your connection to homeland conflict. (*If they need a prompt—for example, experiencing reception or discrimination*)

Question #18: Is there anything about America's historical and/or current involvement in the Israeli-Palestinian conflict that is important for how you personally relate to it as a Palestinian/Israeli American?

Question #19: Is there anything about the mass media coverage of the conflict that matters for how you personally relate to it as a Palestinian/Israeli American?

Question #20: Do you feel that the United States has been supportive of Palestinians and/or Jewish-Israelis? If not, do you think that your connection to the homeland conflict would be different if you lived in a pro-Palestinian and/or pro-Jewish-Israeli nation? If yes, in what ways?

Question #21: As of right now, what do you predict to be the future of the conflict?

<u>*Question #22*</u>: What do you think is the best solution for resolving the conflict?

<u>*Question #23*</u>: Do you think that there's a difference between what first generation Israelis/Palestinians and second generation Israelis/Palestinians see as the best solution for resolving the conflict?

<u>*Question #24*</u>: Do you think that there's a difference between what Israeli Americans/Palestinian Americans and non-Israeli Jewish Americans/non-Palestinian Arab Americans see as the best solution for resolving the conflict?

<u>*Question #25*</u>: Do you think that there's a difference between what Israeli Americans/Palestinian Americans and Palestinian Americans/Israeli Americans see as the best solution for resolving the conflict?

<u>*Question #26*</u>: Is there anything we haven't discussed that you would like to add?

Appendix B: A personal reflection on the research process and the conflict

I thought it important to speak not just about the ethnic identities of my subjects, but also about my own Jewish identity (as a partial "Insider") and how it transformed through the process of conducting this study. I came across many new perspectives and facts in my initial literature search to see what others had to say about issues of the Israeli-Palestinian conflict and identity. I had more direct experience with Jewish Israelis, and it was only through reading the words of Palestinians themselves (such as Edward Said, Sarah Roy, and Rashid Khalidi) that I began to understand the other half of the story I had been told since early childhood. Having always heard the traditional Jewish story—of discovering land without a people and making the desert come alive—I was obviously disconcerted by Palestinian claims that there had been tribes living in well-established Arab villages there for thousands of years.

As I read further, my fuzzy image and detached understanding of life for Palestinians in the occupied territories grew clearer, and the faceless millions I had refrained from deeply considering became real people who were clearly suffering. I had always empathized with both sides of the Israeli-Palestinian conflict; however, I was beginning to gain a much deeper understanding of the complex and contradictory explanations surrounding contested topics such as suicide bombings, the erection of security walls along the West Bank, diasporic Palestinian rights, Jewish fears of losing authority and control of what they believe to be their sole safe haven, and the limited freedoms of Palestinians living in the occupied territories.

When I began the actual process of interviewing Palestinian and Jewish Israeli Americans, talking to them directly about their experiences with and opinions on the conflict in their shared homeland, my connection with this globally-important conflict became all the more real and intense—as did my sense of compassion for those involved. I witnessed several Palestinians—women and men—cry as I probed them to speak in detail about the loss of their family homes or family members. Safia's weeping as she told me about the visits her family made to their now-occupied house in Palestine is a moment I still replay in my mind. I listened as Maytal discussed how she feels torn because living in Israel—where her heart and family are—means always having to rush through the mall with her daughter for fear that a suicide bomber might attack. Hearing this was heart-wrenching, as was listening to Tziporah's stories about her childhood experiences hiding in bomb shelters during the Yom Kippur War.

All of the individuals I interviewed were incredibly kind and willing to share with me innermost thoughts and feelings about what was clearly a very emotional and important part of their lives. Even several years later, I can still clearly see their faces and hear them speak their words. They each had a major impact on me and my own identity as a Jewish American.

Through my research and interviewing processes, I came to realize how incredibly multifaceted and complicated the conflict is, and how achieving peace will involve a very difficult process of negotiation, reparation, and mutual sacrifice. I am now able to see the situation more objectively and to feel compassion for both sides and their suffering. I can also see that, rather than being polar opposites with nothing in common as media-derived stereotyping can lead us to believe, at the most intimate and basic level Palestinians and Jewish Israelis have the same desires and goals—to live freely and in peace. As Hassan put it:

> …[T]here is a chance for peace. Everyone wants to make a living. Everybody wants to secure the future of their children. Everybody wants to make sure that their children have enough to eat, have an education, flourish, make money, live a good life, like my dad wanted for us.

This elemental factor is one that gives me great hope for peace, and the recognition of it is itself perhaps in part a solution to the conflict. I believe that if more people on both sides of the conflict (especially leaders not motivated by self-interests but truly dedicated to a peaceful and fair resolution) created an open dialogue and exchange, tensions and prejudices could be abated, and a land that recognizes both peoples' needs and rights to a nation could be achieved. Based on what I've learned in this study, it is my opinion that true equality can only be achieved with Palestinians and Jewish Israelis having equal rights in a democratic, shared nation. I see Safia's transformation—from fearing Jews and Israelis, to experiencing mutually-felt kinship with Israeli mothers in a peace activist group she co-founded—as a wonderful example of how enduring, positive, immediate encounters with the supposed Other have the potential to assuage hatred and fear, eliminate perceptions of threat, and promote an end to a long-standing conflict.

Table 1:
Description Characteristics for Entire Sample (N = 29)

	Jewish Israeli Americans		Palestinian Americans	
	First Generation (9)	**Second Generation (6)**	**First Generation (5)**	**Second Generation (9)**
Mean Age	**40.9**	**25.5**	**45**[15]	**33.6**
Sex				
Male	4 (44%)	3 (50%)	4 (80%)	5 (56%)
Female	5 (56%)	3 (50%)	1 (20%)	4 (44%)
Married				
Yes	8 (89%)	2[16] (33%)	5 (100%)	4 (44%)
No	1 (11%)	4 (67%)	0	5 (56%)
Children				
Yes	7 (avg. of 2.4)[17]	0	5 (avg. of 3)	4 (avg. of 4)
No	2	6	0	5
Education (average level)	17.4 years	17 years	17 years	15.7 years
Religion				
Jewish	8 (89%)	3 (50%)		
Muslim			4 (80%)	6 (67%)
Christian				2 (22%)
Other				
Non-practicing	1 (11%)	3 (50%)	1 (20%)	1 (11%)

[15] Safia did not reveal her actual age but said she was "30-something." I averaged her age as 35 to get the sample mean.
[16] Sasha identified her partner as her spouse.
[3] Liat was pregnant with her first child.

Table 1 (Continued): Description Characteristics for Entire Sample (N = 29)

	Jewish Israeli Americans		Palestinian Americans	
Frequency of Contact with People in Homeland				
Several Times a Week	5 (56%)	1 (17%)	1 (20%)	0
Once a Week	3 (33%)	0	2 (40%)	0
Few Times a Year	1 (11%)	5 (83%)	2 (40%)	9 (100%)
Frequency of Contact with Ethnic Group Members Here				
Several Times a Week	6 (67%)	5 (83%)	5 (100%)	8 (89%)
Once a Week	2 (22%)	0	0	1 (11%)
Few Times a Year	1 (11%)	1 (17%)	0	0
Number of Homeland Visits (Since Migration)				
0-5		1 (17%)	1 (20%)	7 (78%)
6-10	3 (33%)	4 (66%)	1 (20%)	2 (22%)
11 or more	6 (67%)	1 (17%)	3 (60%)	

Table 1 (Continued): Description Characteristics for Entire Sample (N = 29)

	Jewish Israeli Americans		Palestinian Americans	
Identifies Country of Origin as their Main Homeland	9 (100%)	1 (17%)	5 (100%)	8 (89%)
Sees Homeland Conflict as Main Homeland Issue	9 (100%)	5 (83%)	5 (100%)	9 (100%)

References

Ackerman, S. (2001).Al-Aqsa intifada and the U.S. media."*Journal of Palestine Studies*, 30(2), 61-74.

Ariyanto, A., Hornsey, M.J., &Gallois, C. (2007). Group allegiances and perceptions of media bias: Taking into account both the perceiver and the source. *Group Processes & Intergroup Relations,* 10(2), 266-279.

Barghouti, I. (1988). Palestinian Americans: socio-political attitudes of Palestinian Americans towards the Arab-Israeli conflict, Working Paper. University of Durham, Centre for Middle Eastern and Islamic Studies, Durham, England.

Barth, F. (1969).*Ethnic groups and boundaries: The social organization of culture difference*. Boston, MA: Little, Brown & Company.

Beim, A. (2007). The cognitive aspects of collective memory. *Symbolic Interaction*, 30(1), 7-26.

Ben-Moshe, D. (2007). Chapter 1: The new anti-Semitism, Jewish identity and the question of Zionism. In D. Ben-Moshe & Z. Segev (Eds.), *Israel, the Diaspora and Jewish Identity* (pp. 9-22). Portland, OR: Sussex Academic Press.

Ben-Ze'ev, E. (2005). Chapter 5: Transmission and transformation: The Palestinian second generation and the commemoration of the homeland. In A. Levy & A. Weingrod (Eds.), *Homelands and diasporas: Holy lands and other places* (pp. 123-139). Stanford, CA: Stanford University Press.

Berezin, M. (1997). *Making the fascist self: The political culture of interwar Italy*. Ithaca, NY: Cornell University Press.

Bishara, A. (2008). Watching US television from the Palestinian street: The media, the state, and representational interventions. *Cultural Anthropology*, 23(3), 488-530.

Bonilla-Silva, E. (2003). *Racism without racists: Color-blind racism and the persistence of racial inequality in the United States.* Lanham, MD: Rowan & Littlefield Publishers, Inc. Brodkin, K. (1998). *How Jews became white folks and what that says about race in America.* New Brunswick, NJ: Rutgers University Press.

Brubaker, R. (2005). The 'diaspora' diaspora. *Ethnic and Racial Studies*, 28(1), 1-19.

Brubaker, R. & Cooper, F. (2000).Beyond 'identity.' *Theory and Society*, 29(1), 1-47.

Bruner, J.S. (1990). *Acts of meaning.* Cambridge, MA: Harvard University Press.

Burke, P. (1989). History as social memory. In T. Butler (Ed.), *Memory: History, culture and the mind* (pp. 97-113). New York, NY: Blackwell.

Cainkar, L. (2009). *Homeland insecurity: The Arab American and Muslim American experience after 9/11.* New York, NY: Russell Sage Foundation.

Caldwell, D. (2002). The rapture factor: why conservative Christians' love of Israel is intertwined with the Battle of Armageddon. Retrieved from http://www.beliefnet.com/Faiths/Christianity/2002/06/The-Rapture-Factor.aspx?p=1

Calhoun, C. (1994). Social theory and the politics of identity. In C. Calhoun (Ed.), *Social theory and the politics of identity* (pp. 9-36). Cambridge, MA: Blackwell.

Carter, Jimmy. (2006). *Palestine: Peace not apartheid.* New York, NY: Simon & Schuster.

Chamberlain, M., &Leydesdorff, S. (2004). Transnational families: memories and narratives. *Global Networks*, 4(3), 227-241.

Chomsky, N. (1999). *The fateful triangle: The United States, Israel, and the Palestinians.* Boston, MA: South End Press.

Chomsky, N. (2010). *Hopes and prospects.* Chicago, IL: Haymarket Books.

Cohen, R. & Gold, G. (1996). Israelis in Toronto: The myth of return and the development of a distinct ethnic community. *Jewish Journal of Sociology*, 38(1), 17-26.

Connor, P. (2009). International migration and religious participation: The mediating impact of individual and contextual effects. *Sociological Forum*, 24(4), 779-803.

Coser, L. A. (1956).*The functions of social conflict.* London, England: Routledge & Kegan Paul.

Davies, W. D. (1982). *The territorial dimension of Judaism.* Berkeley, CA: University of California Press.

Dhunpath, R. (2000). Life history methodology: "narradigm" regained. *International Journal of Qualitative Studies in Education*, 13(5), 543-551.

Don-Yehiya, E. (1998). Zionism in retrospective. *Modern Judaism*, 18(3), 267-276.

Dunsky, M. (2008). *Pens and swords: How the American mainstream media report the Israeli-Palestinian conflict.* New York, NY: Columbia University Press.

Durham County. U.S. Census Bureau American Fact Finder. Retrieved December 11, 2010 from http://factfinder.census.gov/home/saff/main.html?_lang=en

Easthope, H. (2009). Fixed identities in a mobile world? The relationship between mobility, place, and identity. *Identities*, 16(1), 61-82.

Eastmond, M. (2007). Stories as lived experience: Narratives in forced migration research. *Journal of Refugee Studies*, 20(2), 248-264.

El-Aswad, E. (2006).The dynamics of identity reconstruction among Arab communities in the United States. *Anthropos*, 101(1), 111-121.

Ellis, M. H. (2002). *Israel and Palestine out of the ashes: The search for Jewish identity in the twenty-first century.* London, England: Pluto Press.

Ellis, M. H. (2009). *Judaism does not equal Israel.* New York, NY: New Press.

Ellis, M., &Almgren, G. (2009).Local contexts of immigrant and second-generation integration in the United States. *Journal of Ethnic and Migration Studies*, 35(7), 1059-1076.

Esposito, L., & Murphy, J.W. (2000).Another step in the study of race relations. *Sociological Quarterly*, 41(2), 171-187.

Eveland, W. P., Jr., & Shah, D. V. (2003). The impact of individual and interpersonal factors on perceived news media bias. *Political Psychology*, 24, 101-117.

Fivush, R. (2008). Remembering and reminiscing: How individual lives are constructed in family narratives. *Memory Studies*, 1(1), 49-58.

Foner, N. (2009). Migration, location and memory: Jewish history through a comparative lens. In D. Cesarani, T. Kushner, & M. Shain (Eds.), *Place and Displacement in Jewish History and Memory* (pp. 131-140). London, England: Vallentine Mitchell.

Gans, H.J. (2007). Ethnic and Racial Identity. In M.C. Waters & R. Ueda (Eds.), *The New Americans: A Guide to Immigration Since 1965* (pp. 98-109). Cambridge, MA: Harvard University Press.

Gaza Strip. CIA world factbook. Retrieved December 1, 2010 from https://www.cia.gov/library/publications/the-world-factbook/geos/gz.html

Geertz, C. (1973). *The interpretation of cultures: Selected Essays*. New York, NY: Basic Books.

Georgiou, Myria. (2006). *Diaspora, identity and the media: Diasporic transnationalism and mediated specialties*. Cresskill, NJ: Hampton Press, Inc.

Gerber, H. (2003). Zionism, orientalism, and the Palestinians. *Journal of Palestine Studies*, 33(1), 23-41.

Gilens, M. (1999).*Why Americans hate welfare: Race, media, and the politics of antipoverty policy*. Chicago, IL: University of Chicago Press.

Gillespie, M. (2006). Transnational television audiences after September 11. *Journal of Ethnic and Migration Studies*, 32(6), 903-921.

Gold, S.J. (1997). Transnationalism and vocabularies of motive in international migration: The case of Israelis in the United States. *Sociological Perspectives*, 40(3), 409-427.

Gold, S.J. (2002). *The Israeli Diaspora*. Seattle, WA: University of Washington Press.

Gold, S.J. (2007). Chapter 10: The Place of Israel in the Identity of Israelis in the Diaspora: An Ethnographic Exploration. In D. Ben-Moshe & Z. Segev (Eds.), *Israel, the Diaspora and Jewish Identity* (pp. 185-205). Portland, OR: Sussex Academic Press.

Gold, S.J. &Bozorgmehr, M. (2007).Middle East and North Africa.In M.C. Waters & R. Ueda (Eds.), *The New Americans: A Guide to Immigration Since 1965* (pp. 518-533). Cambridge, MA: Harvard University Press.

Gowricharn, R. (2009). Changing forms of transnationalism. *Ethnic and Racial Studies*, 32(9), 1619-1638.

Gur-Ze'ev, I., &Pappé, I. (2003). Beyond the destruction of the other's collective memory: Blueprints for a Palestinian/Israeli dialogue. *Theory, Culture & Society*, 20(1), 93-108.

Grossman, D. (1993). *Sleeping on a wire: Conversations with Palestinians in Israel*. New York, NY: Farrar, Straus, and Giroux.

Halbwachs, M. (1992).*On Collective Memory* (L.A. Coser, Ed. & Trans.).Chicago, IL: University of Chicago Press. (Original work published 1925)

Haller, W. &Landolt, P. (2005). The transnational dimensions of identity formation: Adult children of immigrants in Miami." *Ethnic and Racial Studies*, 28(6), 1182-214.

Hammer, J. (2005). *Palestinians born in exile: Diaspora and the search for a homeland.* Austin, TX: University of Texas Press.

Hanafi, S. (2005). Chapter 4: Rethinking the Palestinians abroad as a diaspora: The relationship between the diaspora and the Palestinian territories. In A. Levy & A. Weingrod (Eds.), *Homelands and diasporas: Holy lands and other places* (pp. 97-122). Stanford, CA: Stanford University Press.

Hobsbawm, E.J. (1972). The social function of the past: some questions. *Past Present*, 55, 3-17.

Hogan, M. (2001). The 1948 massacre at DeirYassin revisited. *Historian*, 63(2), 309.

Huttunen, L. (2005). 'Home' and ethnicity in the context of war: Hesitant diasporas of Bosnian refugees. *European Journal of Cultural Studies*, 8(2), 177-195.

Israel. CIA world factbook. Retrieved December 1, 2010 from https://www.cia.gov/library/publications/the-world-factbook/geos/is.html

Jenkins, R. (2008). *Social identity* (3rd ed.). New York, NY: Routledge.

Kamalipour, Y.R. (Ed). (1997). *The U.S. media and the Middle East: Image and perception.* Westport, CT: Praeger.

Kaplan, E. (2005). *The Jewish radical right: Revisionist Zionism and its ideological legacy*. Madison: The University of Wisconsin Press.

Kasinitz, P., Waters, M.C., Mollenkopf, J.H., & Anil, M. (2002). Chapter 3: Transnationalism and the children of immigrants in contemporary New York. In P. Levitt & M.C. Waters (Eds.), *The changing face of home: The transnational lives of the second generation* (pp. 96-122). New York, NY: Russell Sage Foundation.

Katriel, T. (2009).Inscribing Narratives of Occupation in Israeli Popular Memory. In M. Keren& H.H. Herwig (Eds.), *War memory and popular culture: Essays on modes of remembrance and commemoration* (pp. 150-165). Jefferson, NC: McFarland & Company, Inc., Publishers. Keightley, E. (2010). Remembering research: Memory and methodology in the social sciences.*International Journal of Social Research Methodology*, 13(1), 55-70.

Khalidi, R. (1997). *Palestinian identity: The construction of modern national consciousness*. New York, NY: Columbia University Press.

Khalili, L. (2005). Virtual nation: Palestinian cyberculture in Lebanese camps. In R.L.Stein & T. Swedenburg (Eds.), *Palestine, Israel and the politics of popular culture* (pp. 126-149). Durham, NC: Duke University Press.

Kibria, N. (2002). Chapter 12: Of blood, belonging, and homeland trips: Transnationalism and identity among second-generation Chinese and Korean Americans. In P. Levitt & M.C. Waters (Eds.), *The changing face of home: The transnational lives of the second generation* (pp. 295-311). New York, NY: Russell Sage Foundation.

Korostelina, K.V. (2007). *Social identity and conflict: Structures, dynamics, and implications*. New York, NY: PALGRAVE MACMILLAN.

Langfield, M. (2009).'Lost worlds': Reflections on home and belonging in Jewish Holocaust survivor testimonies. In D. Cesarani, T. Kushner, & M. Shain (Eds.), *Place and displacement in Jewish history and memory* (pp. 29-42). London: Vallentine Mitchell.

Lamont, M. & Molnar, V. (2002). The study of boundaries in the social sciences. *Annual Review of Sociology*, 28(1), 167-195.

Lentin, R. (2009). Memories for the future. *International Sociology*, 24(2), 173-84.

Levinson, D. & Ember, M. (Eds.). (1997). *American immigrant cultures: Builders of a nation* (Vol. 2). New York, NY: Simon & Schuster Macmillan.

Levitt, P. (2001). *The transnational villagers*. Berkeley, CA: University of California Press.

Levitt, P. (2009). Roots and routes: Understanding the lives of the second generation transnationally. *Journal of Ethnic and Migration Studies*, 35(7), 1225-1242.

Levitt, P., &Jaworsky, N.B. (2007). Transnational migration studies: Past developments and future trends. *Annual Review of Sociology*, 33(1), 129-156.

Levitt, P. & Waters, M.C. (2002).Introduction. In P. Levitt & M.C. Waters (Eds.), *The changing face of home: The transnational lives of the second generation* (pp. 1-12). New York, NY: Russell Sage Foundation.

McAdams, D.P., Diamond, A., de St. Aubin, E, & Mansfield, E. (1997). Stories of commitment: The psychosocial construction of generative lives. *Journal of Personality and Social Psychology*, 72(3), 678-694.

MacIntyre, A.C. (2007). *After virtue: A study in moral theory* (3rd ed.). Notre Dame, IN: University of Notre Dame Press.

Mannheim, K. (1952). *Essays on the sociology of knowledge*. London, England: Routledge & Kegan Paul.

Marvasti, A.B. & McKinney, K.D. (2004). *Middle Eastern lives in America*. Lanham, MD: Rowan & Littlefield Publishers, Inc.

Matar, D. (2006). Diverse diasporas, one meta-narrative: Palestinians in the UK talking about 11 September 2001. *Journal of Ethnic and Migration Studies*, 32(6), 1027-1040.

Memmi, A. (1965). *The colonizer and the colonized*. Boston, MA: Beacon Press.

Merton, R.K. (1972). Insiders and outsiders: A chapter in the sociology of knowledge. *American Journal of Sociology*, 78(1): 9-47.

Metro Area Membership Report. The Association of Religion Data Archives. Retrieved December 14, 2010 from http://www.thearda.com/mapsReports/reports/metro/6640_2000.asp

Misztal, B.A. (2010). Collective memory in a global age: Learning how and what to remember. *Current Sociology*, 58(1), 24-44.

Nagel, J. (1996). *American Indian ethnic renewal: Red power and the resurgence of identity and culture*. New York, NY: Oxford University Press.

Nets-Zehngut, R. (2008).The Israeli national information center and collective memory of the Israeli-Arab conflict.*TheMiddle East Journal*, 62(4), 653-670.

Noakes, J.A., & Gwinn, K.G. (2002).Shifting frames of the Palestinian movement in US news.*Media, Culture & Society*, 24(5), 649-671.

Olick, J.K. (1999). Collective memory: The two cultures. *Sociological Theory*, 17(3), 333-348.

Olick, J.K. (2008). Collective memory: A memoir and a prospect. *Memory Studies*, 1(1), 23-29.

Olick, J.K. & Robbins, J. (1998). Social memory studies: From "collective memory" to the historical sociology of mnemonic practices. *Annual Review of Sociology*, 24(1), 105-140.

Olzak, S. (1992).*The dynamics of ethnic competition and conflict.* Stanford, CA: Stanford University Press.

Olzak, S. & Nagel, J. (Eds.).(1986). *Competitive ethnic relations.* Orlando, FL: Academic Press.

Orange County. U.S. Census Bureau American Fact Finder. Retrieved December 11, 2010 from http://factfinder.census.gov/home/saff/main.html?_lang=en

Orbuch, T.L. (1997). People's accounts count: The sociology of accounts. *Annual Review of Sociology,* 23(1), 455-478.

Patterson, R. (2006). Transnationalism: Diaspora-homeland development. *Social Forces*, 84(4), 1891-1907.

Peled, Y. (1992). Ethnic democracy and the legal construction of citizenship: Arab citizens of the Jewish State. *American Political Science Review*, 86(2), 432-443.

Portes, A., Fernandez-Kelly, P., & Haller, W. (2009). The adaptation of the immigrant second generation in America: A theoretical overview and recent evidence. *Journal of Ethnic and Migration Studies*, 35(7), 1077-1104.

Portes, A. &Rumbaut, R.G. (2005). Introduction: The second generation and the children of immigrants longitudinal study. *Ethnic and Racial Studies*, 28(6), 983-999.

Portes, A. &Rumbaut, R.G. (2006).*Immigrant America: A portrait* (3rd ed.). Berkeley, CA: University of California Press.

Ram, U. (2009). Ways of forgetting: Israel and the obliterated memory of the Palestinian nakba. *Journal of Historical Sociology*, 22(3), 366-395.

Rebhun, U. & Lev Ari, L. (2010). *American Israelis: Migration, transnationalism, and diasporic identity*. Lieden, The Netherlands: Brill.

Reich, B. (1991). Themes in the history of the State of Israel. *American Historical Review*, 96(5), 1466-1478.

Roy, S. (1995). *The Gaza strip: The political economy of de-development*. Washinton, DC: Institute for Palestine Studies.

Rumbaut, R.G. (2002). Chapter 2: Severed or sustained attachments? Language, identity, and imagined communities in the post-immigrant generation. In P. Levitt & M.C. Waters (Eds.), *The changing face of home: The transnational lives of the second generation* (pp. 43-95). New York, NY: Russell Sage Foundation.

Said, E.W. (1979).*The question of Palestine*. New York, NY: Times Books.

Sakr, N. (1999). Satellite television and development in the Middle East. *Middle East Report*, 210. Retrieved from http://www.merip.org/index.html

Schuman H. & Scott, J. (1989).Generations and collective memory. *American Sociological Review*, 54(3), 359-381.

Schwartz, B. (1996). Memory as a cultural system: Abraham Lincoln in World War II. *American Sociological Review*, 61(5), 908-927.

Shain, Y. (1996). Arab-Americans at a crossroads. *Journal of Palestine Studies,* 25(3), 47-59.

Shamir, M., &Sagiv-Schifter, T. (2006). Conflict, identity, and tolerance: Israel in the Al-Aqsa intifada. *Political Psychology*, 27(4), 569-595.

Sharp, J.M. (2010, September 16). *U.S. foreign aid to Israel*. Retrieved from http://www.fas.org/sgp/crs/mideast/RL33222.pdf

Siapera, E. (2010). *Cultural diversity and global media: The mediation of difference*. West Sussex, England.Wiley-Blackwell.

Simmel, G. (1955). *Conflict and the web of group affiliations* (K. Wolff, Ed. & Trans.).Glencoe, IL: Free Press.

Slater, J. (2007). Muting the alarm over the Israeli-Palestinian conflict.*International Security*, *32*(2), 84-120.

Smooha, S. (1998).The implications of the transition to peace for Israeli society. *Annals of the American Academy of Political and Social Science*, 555, 26-46.

State of North Carolina Ancestry Data, 2000 U.S. Census, PCT18 (Ancestry Total Categories Tallied for People with One or More

Ancestry Categories Reported). U.S. Census Bureau American Fact Finder. Retrieved December 11, 2010 from http://factfinder.census.gov/home/saff/main.html?_lang=en

Stein, R.L. & Swedenburg, T. (Eds). 2005. *Palestine, Israel and the politics of popular culture*. Durham, NC: Duke University Press.

Stepick, A., & Stepick, C.D. (2010).The complexities and confusions of segmented assimilation. *Ethnic and Racial Studies*, 33(7), 1149-1167.

Stets, J.E., Burke, P.J. (2000).Identity theory and social identity theory. *Social Psychology Quarterly*, 63(3), 224-237.

Sztokman, E. (2007). Gender and Israel in diaspora Jewish identity. In D. Ben-Moshe & Z. Segev (Eds.), *Israel, the Diaspora and Jewish Identity* (pp. 164-175). Portland, OR: Sussex Academic Press.

Talbot, S. (2008). 'Us' and 'them': Terrorism, conflict and (O)ther discursive formations. *Sociological Research Online*, 13(1/2), 18.

Tilly, C. (2002). *Stories, identities, and political change*. Lanham, MD: Rowan & Littlefield Publishers, Inc.

Trew, J.D. (2010). Reluctant diasporas of Northern Ireland: Migrant narratives of home, conflict, difference. *Journal of Ethnic and Migration Studies*, 36(4), 541-560.

Uslaner, E.M., Canetti-Nissim, D. &Pedazhur, A. (2004). Terrorism and trust: Sustained violence and the social fabric in Israel, Unpublished manuscript, University of Maryland, College Park, MD & Haifa University, Haifa, Israel.

United States Membership Report. The Association of Religion Data Archives. Retrieved December 14, 2010 from http://www.thearda.com/mapsReports/reports/US_2000.asp

Viswanath, K. &Ka-man Lee, K. (2007). Ethnic Media. In M.C. Waters & R. Ueda (Eds.), *The new Americans: A guide to immigration since 1965* (pp. 202-213). Cambridge, MA: Harvard University Press.

Wake County. U.S. Census Bureau American Fact Finder. Retrieved December 11, 2010 from http://factfinder.census.gov/home/saff/main.html?_lang=en

Wald, K.D. (2009). The diaspora project of Arab Americans: Assessing the magnitude and determinants of politicized ethnic identity. *Ethnic and Racial Studies*, 32(8), 1304-1324.

Waldinger, R. & Fitzgerald, D. (2004). Transnationalism in question. *American Journal of Sociology*, 109(5), 1177-1195.

Waldorf, B. (1995). Determinants of international return migration intentions. *Professional Geographer*, 47(2), 125.

Waters, M.C.& Ueda, R. (2007). Introduction. In M.C. Waters & R. Ueda (Eds.), *The new Americans: A guide to immigration since 1965* (pp. 1-13). Cambridge, MA: Harvard University Press.

Waters, M.C., Tran, V.C., Kasinitz, P., & Mollenkopf, J.H. (2010). Segmented assimilation revisited: Types of acculturation and socioeconomic mobility in young adulthood. *Ethnic and Racial Studies*, 33(7), 1168-93.

West Bank. CIA world factbook. Retrieved December 1, 2010 from https://www.cia.gov/library/publications/the-world-factbook/geos/we.html

Worchel, S. (2005). Culture's role in conflict and conflict management: Some suggestions, many questions. *International Journal of Intercultural Relations*, 29(6), 739-757.

Yerushalmi, Y.H. (1982). *Zakhor: Jewish history and Jewish memory*. Seattle, WA: University of Washington Press.

Zelizer, B. (1995). Reading the past against the grain: the shape of memory studies. *Critical Studies in Mass Communication*, 12(2), 214-239.

Zerubavel, E. (1996). Social memories: Steps to a sociology of the past. *Qualitative Sociology*, 19(3), 283-300.

Zhou M. (1997).Growing up American: The challenge confronting immigrant children and children of immigrants. *Annual Review Sociology*, 23(1), 63-96.

Zimmermann, L., Zimmermann, K.F. & Constant, A. (2007).Ethnic self-identification of first-generation immigrants. *International Migration Review*, 41(3), 769-781.

Index

Index